The Regulation of Pharmaceuticals

Balancing the Benefits and Risks

Henry G. Grabowski
John M. Vernon

American Enterprise Institute for Public Policy Research
Washington and London

Henry Grabowski and John Vernon, both professors of economics at Duke University, have written a number of studies analyzing the effects of regulation in pharmaceuticals and other industries. Their collaborative work includes *The Impact of Regulation of Industrial Innovation,* published by the National Academy of Sciences in 1979, as well as many journal articles.

Library of Congress Cataloging in Publication Data

Grabowski, Henry G.
     The regulation of pharmaceuticals.

     (AEI studies ; 377)
        1. Drugs—Law and legislation—United States.
2. Pharmacy—Law and legislation—United States.
3. United States.   Food and Drug Administration.
I. Vernon, John Mitcham, 1937–   .   II. Title.
III. Series.   [DNLM: 1. Drug industry—Standards—
United States.   2. Drugs—Standards.   3. Legislation,
Drug—United States.   4. Research—Standards—
United States.   5. United States—Food and Drug
Administration.   QV 771 G728f]
KF3885.G7   1983   344.73′04233   83–2648
ISBN 0–8447–3517–5   347.3044233

AEI Studies 377

Printed in the United States of America

Contents

1
Introduction

Regulation of the pharmaceutical industry dates back to the early part of this century. The system of government controls that has evolved is among the most extensive and stringent for any product class. The regulatory process is centered on the premarket screening of new pharmaceutical agents. All new drug therapies must be approved as safe and effective by the Food and Drug Administration (FDA) before they can be marketed. In addition, there are significant regulatory controls over the clinical research process, over the labeling and promotion of drug therapies, and over laboratory and manufacturing practices.

Many of these controls stem from the passage of the 1962 Kefauver-Harris amendments to the Food, Drug, and Cosmetic Act and the regulations issued by the FDA in implementing those amendments. Since 1962 there have been a number of adverse trends in pharmaceutical innovation. The annual rate of new chemical entities (NCEs) introduced has fallen, research and development (R and D) costs have risen, and the United States has lagged significantly behind other countries in making new drug therapies available. These trends have led to a great deal of interest in and controversy about regulatory reform at the FDA.

In this introductory chapter we examine the origins and development of the regulatory process in pharmaceuticals. Next we discuss "market failure" as a rationale for government regulation. We then analyze the problems of "nonmarket failure" arising from the FDA's regulatory intervention in a research-intensive innovative industry such as pharmaceuticals.

Historical Background of Food and Drug Regulation

The first law regulating pharmaceuticals was the Pure Food and Drug Act of 1906, which prohibited adulteration and mislabeling of food and drugs sold in interstate commerce.[1] The law was passed in the progressive era of President Theodore Roosevelt's administration and was largely a response to publicity generated by Upton Sinclair's *The Jungle* and the works of other muckrakers of that era. At the time of passage, there were no constraints on the sale of pharmaceuticals to consumers (such as the need to obtain a physician's prescription), and prescription drugs constituted less than a third of all drugs consumed. Many patent medicines with extensive medical claims but of doubtful value were being sold.

The 1906 law and a subsequent amendment in 1912 were designed to correct such patent medicine abuses by prohibiting false or misleading claims. The law was generally ineffective in accomplishing this objective because initially only a very small staff of chemists was available for enforcement and, more significantly, because a series of court decisions put the burden on the government to demonstrate fraud in prosecuting producers making unproven claims for their products. The law did allow the FDA to remove from the market some products whose contents were incorrectly represented as well as some products involving obvious fraud.

During the first term of President Franklin Roosevelt, legislation was introduced to strengthen the powers of the FDA. It was not until 1938, however, after a major drug disaster involving the drug sulfanilamide, that new legislation was passed by Congress. In attempting to formulate a liquid form of sulfanilamide, a major sulfa drug, the Massengill Company created an elixir that used diethylene glycol as a solvent without testing it for toxicity. More than a hundred children died from this liquid combination because diethylene glycol turned out to be a poisonous chemical.

After this drug disaster, Congress passed the Food, Drug, and Cosmetic Act of 1938, which required firms to submit a new drug application (NDA) to the FDA before introducing any new pharmaceutical into interstate commerce. The application had to enumerate the uses of the drug and demonstrate that it was safe under the recommended conditions. The application was automatically approved in sixty days unless the secretary of agriculture (under whose jurisdiction the FDA rested at the time) determined that it did not contain sufficient tests of drug safety. The law also provided the basis for subsequent FDA regulations that separated pharmaceuticals into ethical drugs, which may be purchased only with a physician's prescription, and proprietary drugs, which may be sold over the counter to all consumers.[2]

Despite these new regulatory controls, innovation in ethical drugs flourished over the next two decades. Many major advances were achieved, including the introduction of antibiotics (penicillin, tetracyclines), tranquilizers, antihypertensives, diuretics, and antidiabetic agents. Competition in the drug industry increasingly focused on the discovery and development of new chemical entities. Total industry R and D expenditures increased dramatically along with the volume of NCEs.

Although the premarket safety reviews of the FDA obviously caused time lags in introducing NCEs and kept some drugs out of the marketplace, regulatory review times were still quite short (seven months on average), and the annual volume of NCEs introduced was at record levels (over fifty per year) at the end of the 1950s. Indeed, the focus of congressional oversight committees in this period turned to the high profits earned by some prescription drugs and to company patents and trademarks as the source of above-average profits. Senator Estes Kefauver held a number of hearings on this issue and attempted to get Congress to pass legislation designed to curb these perceived competitive abuses through compulsory licensing of drug patents and prohibition of separate brand names for prescription drugs.

Senator Kefauver was unsuccessful in gaining legislative support for these economic-oriented policy changes. A major regulatory bill was passed in 1962 under his sponsorship, however: the Kefauver-Harris amendments to the Food, Drug, and Cosmetic Act. This law passed after the well-known and tragic events associated with thalidomide. This drug, which produced fetal deformities in pregnant women, had been introduced in several European countries but not in the United States, where its introduction had been delayed by an FDA investigation. The large-scale media publicity about thalidomide's toxic properties caused the Kefauver Committee to shift its focus from economic to safety concerns. The 1962 amendments were then quickly drafted and passed with little opposition by Congress.

Two basic provisions of the amendments directly affected the process of drug innovation—a proof-of-efficacy requirement for approval of new drugs and establishment of FDA regulatory controls over the clinical (human) testing of new drug candidates.

The amendments required firms to provide substantial evidence of a new drug's efficacy based on "adequate and well controlled trials." Subsequent FDA regulations interpreted this provision to mean the use of experimental and control groups to demonstrate a drug's efficacy as statistically significant. The preferred mode of study was "double blind" control, where neither patient nor physician knew whether the patient was receiving the experimental drug or a standard therapy or placebo. According to industry sources, the FDA's regulations concerning substantial evidence of safety and efficacy led to large increases in the resources necessary to obtain approval of a new drug application (NDA), especially in therapeutic areas where

3

analyses of patients' responses are necessarily subjective (such as analgesics and antidepressants).

The second major change in the 1962 amendments influencing drug innovation was the institution of investigational new drug (IND) requirements for clinical testing. Before any tests on human subjects, firms were required to submit a new drug investigational plan giving the results of animal tests and research protocols for human tests. After evaluating the IND and subsequent reports of research findings, the FDA may prohibit, delay, or halt clinical research that poses excessive risks to volunteer subjects or that does not follow sound scientific procedures. As a result of the IND procedures, the FDA shifted after 1962 from essentially an evaluator of evidence and research findings at the end of the R and D process to an active participant in the process itself. This shift contributed to the higher development costs and longer times for pharmaceutical R and D.

The amendments also repealed the automatic approval of an NDA within 60 days if the FDA did not take action to prevent the drug from reaching the market. The FDA now had to take affirmative action on an NDA for the drug to enter the marketplace. It was supposed to make a decision within 180 days, but no sanctions were provided for longer deliberation times. The law also set into motion the Drug Efficacy Study Implementation (DESI) program to review the effectiveness of drugs on the market under the 1938 statute. Drugs that could not meet the new standards of evidence of efficacy were to be removed from the market by the FDA.

In addition to these regulations regarding proof of safety and efficacy, the law regulated various other aspects of firms' behavior. First, the amendments imposed controls on the advertising and promotion of prescription drugs. They required firms to include generic names on drug labels in addition to brand names and to restrict all advertised claims to those approved by the FDA in labeling and packaging inserts. Second, they required drug firms to adhere to standards of good manufacturing practice, which would be set out in detailed FDA regulations.

The 1962 amendments were thus a culmination of the shift of primary decision-making authority in pharmaceuticals from market mechanisms to a centralized regulatory authority. The early regulatory laws in this area had essentially sought to make the market work better through government provision of information and the elimination of false claims and misinformation. The 1938 and 1962 legislative actions, which followed highly publicized adverse drug incidents, had a very different objective. They sought to protect consumers by barring undesirable products from the market. The judgment about

4

what was desirable or undesirable was to be made by a central regulatory authority rather than by market forces and the voluntary choices of suppliers, physicians, and patients.

After the 1962 legislation, the external environment surrounding FDA decisions on new drug approvals also changed significantly. The thalidomide disaster, widely reported in the popular press, focused the attention of Congress and the media on the potential risks of new drugs.

Former FDA Commissioner Alexander Schmidt has emphasized the problems these external pressures create for the maintenance of balanced and rational decision making at the FDA. As he observed in a speech while commissioner during the mid-1970s:

> For example, in all of FDA's history, I am unable to find a single instance where a Congressional committee investigated the failure of FDA to approve a new drug. But, the times when hearings have been held to criticize our approval of new drugs have been so frequent that we aren't able to count them. . . . The message to FDA staff could not be clearer. Whenever a controversy over a new drug is resolved by its approval, the Agency and the individuals involved likely will be investigated. Whenever such a drug is disapproved, no inquiry will be made. The Congressional pressure for our negative action on new drug applications is, therefore, intense. And it seems to be increasing, as everyone is becoming a self-acclaimed expert on carcinogenesis and drug testing.[3]

In the two decades that have elapsed since more stringent regulation of pharmaceuticals took effect in the early 1960s, pharmaceutical innovation has exhibited a number of adverse trends. These include sharp increases in the R and D costs and the gestation times for NCEs, large declines in the annual rate of NCE introduction for the industry, and a well-publicized lag in the introduction of significant new drug therapies when compared with other developed countries such as the United Kingdom and West Germany. These phenomena are discussed in detail in chapter 3. By the end of the 1960s these adverse trends were becoming readily apparent. A number of research studies linking the more stringent regulatory climate with the higher costs and lower levels of pharmaceutical innovation were published. One particularly well-known study, by Sam Peltzman, also reported that the benefits of the 1962 amendments were small.[4]

These studies sparked considerable debate and controversy among policy makers. Successive FDA administrations attempted to show that other factors besides regulation (such as a depletion of research opportunities) accounted for the slowdown in innovation. They also attempted to minimize or even completely deny the loss of significant therapeutic benefits associated with the lag in NCE introductions.

By the end of the 1970s, however, Congress focused increased attention on the drug lag question and the adverse effects on innovation of the regulatory process. A comprehensive drug reform act initiated by the Carter administration in 1978 had some features designed to reduce drug lag (but also several features that arguably would have operated to slow the process further). This bill failed to receive sufficient support to be enacted.

The concern with drug lag and the adverse incentives to innovation of FDA regulation has continued to intensify. In 1980 the General Accounting Office (GAO) issued a report documenting significant lags in introducing therapies that the FDA itself ranked as important medical advances and pointing out a number of deficiencies in regulatory procedures and in the NCE approval process.[5] Two congressmen, Representatives Fred Scheuer and Albert Gore, initiated a series of hearings on FDA regulatory procedures. Also in 1981 a task force of academic experts, FDA officials, and congressional White House staff representatives was assembled to recommend ways of improving the regulatory process and reducing its adverse effects on innovation.

Although the relation of regulation to innovation in pharmaceuticals remains a complex issue subject to continuing research, there appears to be a growing political consensus that regulation has had significant negative effects on innovation and that some changes in current procedures are desirable. The new administration has given its initial attention to possible changes in FDA regulations rather than legislative changes in the Food, Drug, and Cosmetic Act. Several changes now being proposed are considered in chapter 5.

Market Failure as a Rationale for Drug Regulation

Pharmaceutical agents have frequently been described as two-edged swords. They can be the source of great therapeutic benefits as well as very great risks. Even established drugs of therapeutic choice are not free of risk. Taken in a dosage too low or too high, they can have serious or even fatal consequences. Moreover, the combination of therapeutically beneficial drugs can produce toxic side effects not associated with them individually. And possible idiosyncratic response to pharmaceutical agents—though relatively infrequent or rare—may pose very serious dangers to a small group of patients.

6

The therapeutic benefits and risks of potential new drug entities in very early stages of development are to a high degree uncertain. The uncertainty can be reduced by various tests on animals and people. In an unregulated free-market institution, decisions about how much testing to undertake and when and whether to market a new product would be based on profit incentives. Private profit incentives would be influenced and shaped by various societal institutions, including medical training and the medical delivery system (given the central role of physicians in decisions on drug use), the tort and medical malpractice laws (which set the penalties for product defects and misuse), and patent and product substitution laws (which influence the terms of permissible imitation for new products).

The justification for replacing the forces of the market and its attendant institutions with regulatory authority is generally framed in terms of a "market failure" analysis. The presumed failure is that free-market forces would lead to the introduction and consumption of drug products with excessive risks compared with benefits. This could occur because a supplying firm, to gain the advantages of first introduction or simply to avoid high costs, performed insufficient premarket testing. Firms might also overstate good points and understate negative points in promoting and labeling drugs. Of course, any such tendencies would be constrained to some extent by tort laws as well as by the long-term damage to good repute caused by negative experiences with new drugs.

The source of market failure in this situation is generally called by economists "information imperfection." It is the problem that the customer has in obtaining information about the benefits and risks of new drugs. There are reasons to doubt the completeness of firm-supplied information. Furthermore, because of the "public good" nature of information, it is unlikely that third parties would find it profitable to supply the needed information in sufficient quantity. While such information problems surround many consumer products, the potential threats to human health from the consumption of drugs, which can be severe and irreversible, make them particularly strong candidates for government intervention.

Two alternative strategies for remedying information imperfection are generally available to government policy makers. The first is to try to make the market work better through such measures as government subsidy and provision of information and by altering private incentives to behave in a socially undesirable way (through tort law sanctions and other such penalties). The second is to replace decentralized market decisions with a centralized regulatory control structure so that decisions about premarket tests and market introduction are placed directly in the hands of government officials.

The history of U.S. pharmaceutical regulation is one of steady evolution away from the first strategy—making the market work better—toward the second approach of strong centralized regulatory control over firms' decisions about pharmaceutical testing and marketing. The current system offers a particularly stringent form of product quality regulation, which few other industries, if any, have experienced.

Some have viewed the history of drug regulation as providing convincing evidence of the inadequacies of the first approach and demonstrating the need for strong, centralized regulatory controls. The period from the passage of the 1906 Pure Food and Drug Act to 1938 was characterized by a market-oriented approach—government policing of adulteration and mislabeling of drugs and prosecution of violators through the court system. This approach was insufficient to prevent many market abuses, including the sulfanilamide tragedy, which led directly to the premarket safety reviews of the 1938 legislation.

It can be argued, however, that the ineffectiveness of the early regulatory structure in remedying market imperfections and performance has very limited relevance to the current situation. Early regulation was exclusively directed to sins of commission and had severe constraints placed on it by the congressional mandate and subsequent judicial decisions. Furthermore, there was no government provision of information about new pharmaceuticals and only limited policing of misinformation after the product had been introduced. The market environment for pharmaceuticals was also very different. The vast majority of pharmaceuticals were not dispensed through physicians' prescriptions but were proprietary patent medicines. Furthermore, the tort laws of that period can best be categorized as caveat emptor rather than the extensive and elaborate system of laws dealing with product defects and faults that exists today.

The FDA regulatory program between 1938 and 1962 can be viewed as a blend of the two approaches. The law required premarket application and submission of proof of safety, but approval was automatic after sixty days if the FDA did not raise specific objections. The thrust of regulation during this period seemed oriented to preventing outlier or extreme situations (a few "bad actors"). Most drugs were cleared without major objections by the FDA, and the clearance process seldom took more than several months to complete. The FDA essentially performed a certification role concerning the NDA submission and stood ready to block deficient new drug applications that posed significant safety risks.

The 1962 amendments ushered in a period of strong, centralized regulatory controls over introductions of new drugs and drug product quality. All new drug applications were subject to significantly greater evidentiary standards, requiring proof of safety and efficacy. The approval process became an exhaustive case-by-case review taking two to three years to complete rather than several months. Furthermore, regulatory jurisdiction was extended to the clinical research process, to manufacturing practices, and to the labeling and promotion of drugs. The applicable model for drug regulation therefore apparently shifted from one of dealing with occasional market failure associated with outlier situations or a few "bad actors" to the presumption of a more pervasive and health-threatening market failure that required extensive codification and enforcement of very stringent standards for all new drugs introduced.

Regulatory Failure versus Market Failure

The benefits of government regulation in this and other areas are not costless. The most significant cost of more stringent regulatory controls over introduction of new pharmaceuticals is a slower rate of pharmaceutical innovation.

Ideally, a system of government intervention would give comparable weight to the costs and benefits of regulatory decisions. In practice this is difficult to accomplish. The legislative mandate and regulatory procedures of the FDA evolved as a response to the perceived problems of unsafe or ineffective drugs. Little initial attention was given by Congress or regulators to the potential adverse effects of increased regulation on drug innovation. This asymmetric focus of regulatory officials on the benefits of regulation and relative insensitivity to its costs, a more general phenomenon that has frequently been observed in health and safety regulatory situations, can be a major source of "government failure."

To illustrate the relevance of this point, it is useful to analyze the FDA's regulatory function in terms of a standard statistical decision-making framework (see figure 1). We assume that a new drug application is submitted to the FDA and that some uncertainty exists about whether the drug is safe or effective. The FDA must use the information submitted in the application to make a subjective probability assessment of safety and efficacy and either accept or reject the application. No pharmaceutical is absolutely safe in the sense that it is completely free of adverse side effects. Effectiveness can also vary among patients and clinical situations. Determination

FIGURE 1

FDA DECISION MAKING ON NEW DRUG APPLICATIONS

		State of the world	
		New drug is safe and effective	New drug is not safe and effective
FDA decision	Accept	Correct decision	Type 2 error
	Reject	Type 1 error	Correct decision

SOURCE: Authors.

that a drug is safe and effective is therefore a relative decision involving an informed judgment that therapeutic benefits exceed risks.

In this decision-making situation there are two correct types of decisions and two types of errors. The correct decisions are FDA acceptance of drugs that are safe and effective and rejection of those that are not. Type 1 error is FDA rejection of a "good" drug or one whose benefits would exceed risks in clinical practice. Type 2 error is acceptance of a drug when the reverse is true. Both types of error influence patients' health and well-being since consuming a "bad" drug or not having access to a "good" drug can have deleterious effects on health.

It can be plausibly argued, however, that our regulatory structure does not have a neutral stance between type 1 and type 2 errors. The mandate to the FDA is drawn in very narrow terms—to protect consumers against unsafe or ineffective drugs (that is, to avoid type 2 errors). There is no corresponding mandate to avoid type 1 errors or to compel equal concern with new drug innovation and improved medical therapy. In point of fact, the institutional incentives confronting FDA officials strongly reinforce the tendency to avoid type 2 errors at the expense of type 1 errors. An FDA official who approves a drug subsequently shown to be not safe or effective stands to bear heavy personal costs. Such an outcome, even if it occurs very infrequently, tends to be highly visible and is one for which both the FDA and the regulatory official are held politically accountable. The costs of rejecting a good drug are borne largely by outside parties (drug manufacturers and sick patients who might benefit from it). They are also much less visible. The signals emanating from Congress and the media have tended to reinforce risk avoidance at the FDA. As the earlier quotation from Commissioner Schmidt emphasizes, there have been scores of congressional hearings on controversies over approvals of new drugs, but little attention has been given, at least until very recently, to the FDA's failure to approve new drugs.

One may argue that this analysis is somewhat misleading in that the main effect of the FDA's regulatory behavior is not to prevent useful new therapies from entering the marketplace but rather to delay their introduction. The FDA official may elect to avoid type 2 error not by rejecting a new drug application outright but by opting for more tests before a final decision can be made. By requiring more tests and longer delays, regulators can presumably lower the objective and subjective probability of both type 1 and type 2 errors by obtaining further information from premarket domestic trials and from foreign marketing experience. There are thus strong incentives inherent in the present structure to delay and to increase the number of tests performed before a final decision is reached. At some point, however, one would expect useful new therapies to be approved by the regulatory officials if their domestic and foreign experience is favorable.

The general trade-offs arising from this risk avoidance are depicted further in figure 2. As the required premarket testing increases, the expected R and D costs that must be undertaken for a new drug approval increase in rough proportion. Insofar as the greater testing increases the drug development period, we would also observe delay in the availability of some useful therapies, or "drug lag" costs. At the same time, the expected information about a drug's safety and efficacy also increases with increased testing, so that the expected health costs from the introduction of an unsafe or ineffective drug decline. Because any information so obtained will eventually be subject to sharply diminishing returns, the last curve will tend to flatten out with increased testing while R and D and drug lag costs rise steadily.

Hence, if regulators try to be cautious and avoid type 2 error by ordering more and more resources devoted to premarket testing, they will push firms to the point on these curves where large increments of R and D investments tend to buy very little additional information about safety and efficacy. In short, the FDA might be viewed as being primarily concerned with minimizing expected health costs rather than total costs, thereby setting the level of testing too far to the right in figure 2.

It has also been argued by some critics that inefficiencies in

FIGURE 2
Cost Trade-offs in Premarket Testing

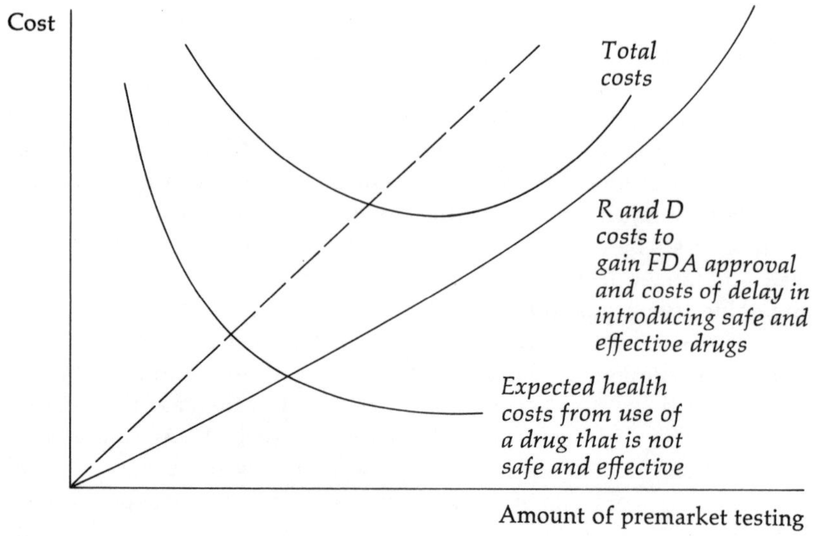

Cost

Total costs

R and D costs to gain FDA approval and costs of delay in introducing safe and effective drugs

Expected health costs from use of a drug that is not safe and effective

Amount of premarket testing

Source: Authors.

interactions between the FDA and firms in the testing process have caused R and D costs to be considerably higher than the minimum feasible level. To the extent that this is true, R and D costs would shift upward as shown by the dashed curve in figure 2.

The long-run consequences of the regulatory behavior depicted in figure 2 will be to increase R and D costs and times above what is socially desirable. This in turn will result in a decline in new drug introductions (or drug loss) because, with higher R and D costs, some potentially beneficial new drugs are no longer profitable or feasible innovations. While it is very difficult to measure the extent of this drug loss since these drugs are never introduced, the loss will tend to be concentrated among drugs with potentially small markets or above-average riskiness to develop. There will thus be forgone health benefits to consumers from the loss of these undeveloped drugs.

We may now summarize the main points of the discussion of market failure and regulatory failure in terms of the analysis presented in figures 1 and 2. Because of the presence of insufficient information incentives and related market imperfections, the unregulated market is seen as prone to insufficient premarket testing (that is, a point too far to the left in figure 2) and consequently to the consumption of too many drugs that are not safe and effective (that is, a type 2 error in figure 1). The incentives and biases associated with our current regulatory regime, however, tend to result in more testing and delay than are socially desirable (that is, a point too far to the right in figure 2). This tends to produce type 1 errors, in which useful drugs are delayed or fail to be introduced at all because of the adverse economic effects of government regulatory decisions and the general insensitivity of the regulatory process to such costs.

In the chapters that follow, we review the empirical evidence concerning the positive and negative effects of FDA pharmaceutical regulation. The final chapter is devoted to a discussion of various proposals that have been advanced in the literature to improve regulatory performance.

Notes

1. For a recent account of the history of drug regulation, see Peter Temin, *Taking Your Medicine: Drug Regulation in the United States* (Cambridge, Mass.: Harvard University Press, 1981). See also William M. Wardell and Louis Lasagna, *Regulation and Drug Development* (Washington, D.C.: American Enterprise Institute, 1975), chap. 1.

2. The prescription-only or ethical drug classification developed out of a relatively minor legislative provision in the 1938 law allowing labeling exemptions. This provides an excellent historical example of how FDA discretion in interpreting the law has been successfully employed by the agency to expand its regulatory controls and authority. See Temin, *Taking Your Medicine*, pp. 46–51.

3. Alexander Schmidt, "The FDA Today: Critics, Congress, and Consumerism," speech delivered before the National Press Club, Washington, D.C., October 29, 1974.

4. Sam Peltzman, *Regulation of Pharmaceutical Innovation: The 1962 Amendments* (Washington, D.C.: American Enterprise Institute, 1974).

5. U.S. General Accounting Office, *FDA Drug Approval—A Lengthy Process That Delays the Availability of Important New Drugs*, HRD-80-64, May 28, 1980.

2
Pharmaceutical Innovation: Basic Characteristics and Regulatory Interventions

In this chapter we discuss various technological and economic aspects of drug discovery and development and the effects of FDA regulation on that process.[1] We begin with a brief discussion of the relation of pharmaceutical innovation to the overall medical care sector.

Social and Economic Effects of New Drug Discoveries

Although the pharmaceutical industry dates from the nineteenth century, its development into a major industry with its current characteristics began only about forty years ago. Before the 1930s the industry was largely commodity based, producing a relatively small number of chemical compounds and engaging in little research or development of new pharmaceuticals.

The present era of the research-oriented pharmaceutical industry began in the mid-1930s, when the first important anti-infective drugs were introduced. Sulfanilamide was introduced in 1936 after it was discovered to be effective against streptococci bacteria without having toxic effects on human cells. This development stimulated considerable interest in research on other potential drug therapies. Several important drugs, most notably penicillin and the other "magic bullet" antibiotics, were introduced over the next decade and a half. After World War II, pharmaceutical research broadened to cover many therapeutic areas. Some of the major discoveries introduced since World War II are synthetic penicillins, tetracyclines, cortisone, chlorpromazine (a major tranquilizer), meprobamate (a minor tranquilizer), antihypertensives, anti-inflammatories, oral contraceptives, diuretics, and antidiabetics.

The revolutionary effects of new drug discoveries on the practice of medicine in this century have been chronicled by a number of

TABLE 1

U.S. Mortality Rates for Selected Diseases, 1960 and 1977
(deaths per 100,000 population)

Disease	1960	1977	Percentage Reduction 1960–1977
Active rheumatic fever and chronic rheumatic heart disease	10.3	5.9	43
Hypertensive heart disease	37.0	4.8	87
Hypertension	7.1	2.6	63
Cerebrovascular diseases	108.0	84.1	22
Arteriosclerosis	20.0	13.3	34
Pneumonia	32.9	23.1	30
Asthma	3.0	0.8	73
Peptic ulcer	6.3	2.7	57
Nephritis and nephrosis	7.6	3.9	49
Kidney infections	4.3	1.7	60
Tuberculosis (all forms)	6.1	1.4	77
Meningitis	1.3	0.7	46
Infectious hepatitis	0.5	0.2	60

Source: *Statistical Abstracts, 1979.*

writers. In his well-known book on health economics *Who Shall Live?* Victor Fuchs has summarized this drug contribution:

> Drugs are the key to modern medicine. Surgery, radiotherapy, and diagnostic tests are all important, but the ability of health care providers to alter health outcomes— Dr. Walsh McDermott's "decisive technology"—depends primarily on drugs. Six dollars are spent on hospitals and physicians for every dollar spent on drugs, but without drugs the effectiveness of hospitals and physicians would be enormously diminished.
>
> The great power of drugs is a development of the twentieth century—many would say of the past forty years. Our age has been given many names—atomic, electronic, space, and the like—but measured by impact on people's lives it might just as well be called the "drug age."[2]

The decline in mortality and morbidity rates associated with major infectious diseases is one of the more striking examples of Fuchs's basic point (see tables 1 and 2). Antibiotics and vaccines have been major factors in the decreases in the incidence of and deaths

TABLE 2
U.S. Cases of Selected Diseases, 1969 and 1978

Disease	1969	1978	Percentage Reduction 1969–1978	Form of Treatment or Prevention
Diphtheria	241	76	68	Vaccines
Encephalitis	1,917	1,183	38	Antibiotics
Measles (all types)	83,542	45,170	46	Vaccines
Meningococcal infections	2,951	2,505	15	Antibiotics
Whooping cough	3,285	2,063	37	Vaccines
Acute rheumatic fever	3,229	851	74	Antibiotics and steroids
Tuberculosis	39,120	28,521	27	Anti-infectives

Source: U.S. Department of Health, Education, and Welfare, Center for Disease Control, *Reported Morbidity and Mortality in the United States, Annual Summary, 1978*, CDC 79-8241, 1979.

from such diseases as tuberculosis, influenza and pneumonia, and poliomyelitis.

New drugs often yield significant benefits as well in the form of a reduced need for hospitalization. Beginning in the 1950s, for example, the pharmaceutical industry introduced a number of therapies that were useful in the treatment of mental illness—tranquilizers and antianxiety and antidepressant drugs. These have had a strong beneficial effect on the amount of hospitalization for mental illness. The population in mental hospitals began to decline for the first time in 1956, two years after the introduction of the first of the major tranquilizers, chlorpromazine. The number of patients declined from 565,485 in 1956 to 202,971 in 1971.

There has been intensified concern in the United States in recent years about the rapid increase in medical care costs and the increasing share of total national resources going to this sector. Figure 3 shows a time plot of the medical care component of the consumer price index (CPI). It has been growing at a significantly greater rate than the CPI for the overall economy. In contrast, the CPI for prescription drugs has advanced by less than half that for the economy as a whole (this is unadjusted for quality changes in pharmaceuticals, which have been substantial over this period). As one might infer from this figure, pharmaceutical costs have accounted for a steadily declining share of the rapidly growing national expenditures on medical costs.

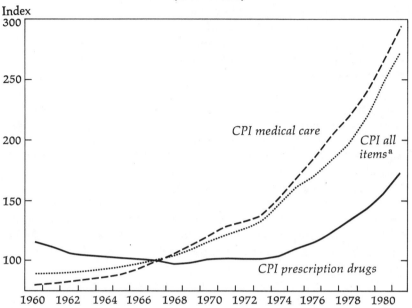

FIGURE 3
SELECTED PRICE INDEXES, 1960–1981
(1967 = 100)

a. CPI(U)–consumer price index for all urban consumers.
SOURCE: U.S. Dept. of Labor, Bureau of Labor Statistics, *Consumer Price Index Detailed Reports*, various issues.

Furthermore, when a new pharmaceutical entity replaces other forms of medical treatment, there are often opportunities for dramatic savings. A recent study by Weisbrod and Geweke, for example, suggests that the antiulcer drug Tagamet, introduced in 1977, has led to significant savings because of the reduced need for surgical treatment of peptic ulcers and for related hospitalization.[3] There are also many historical examples in which pharmaceuticals have replaced more costly modes of treatment with significant gains both therapeutically and in resource savings.

Technological progress in pharmaceuticals, as in other fields, occurs with very different patterns over time and across different product classes. In some cases gains are sharply discontinuous after the introduction of an important new therapy embodying a novel scientific approach. In other cases gains are incremental, each advance building marginally on past introductions. Most "pioneering" drug innovations also spawn a chemically related family of derivative

17

drugs. Some of these later drugs offer significant differences in properties and hence provide decided benefits in comparison to earlier introductions. Others are virtually identical in therapeutic benefits, but many of them still provide economic benefits through the competition they offer to existing entities.

Although the health and economic benefits of past new drug introductions have been substantial, there are obviously many diseases for which existing modes of treatment are unsatisfactory. The three leading causes of death in the United States are heart disease, cancer, and stroke. A recent study by Hartunian and others calculated the direct and indirect costs of cancer in 1975 at $23.1 billion, of heart disease at $13.7 billion, and of stroke at $6.5 billion.[4] The method employed by the authors in this study is, from the standpoint of economic theory, a lower-bound approach, in that there is no attempt to measure and include the personal disutility experienced by persons having these diseases and their families and friends. Nevertheless, the high values observed in the Hartunian study indicate the very great consumer surplus and national resource savings that might be realized by developing better treatments for these and other major diseases.

There is considerable optimism among research scientists about the possibility of developing significant new drug therapies in several of the major disease areas. This optimism is based in considerable part on the great strides that have been made in basic biomedical research over the past decade. At the same time, the economic costs and gestation times for developing and gaining regulatory approval have been moving in a much less desirable direction.

The Drug Discovery Process

The private pharmaceutical industry has been the primary source of discovery of the new chemical entities (NCEs) introduced in recent years (see table 3). It was the originator of approximately 90 percent of all NCEs introduced in the United States since the early 1950s. The source of discovery here is determined by the laboratory of first chemical synthesis and initial demonstration of pharmacological properties. New drug discoveries from industry and nonindustry sources are dependent, in turn, on the stock of biomedical knowledge arising from basic research in university, government, and industry laboratories here and abroad.

New drug competition in the pharmaceutical industry is international, as demonstrated by the data in table 4, which show the country of origin of NCEs introduced in the United States from 1963

TABLE 3

Source of New Chemical Entities Introduced, 1950–1959, 1960–1969, and 1970–1978
(percent)

Source	1950–1959	1960–1969	1970–1978
Pharmaceutical industry	86	91	93
Other	14	9	7
Total	100	100	100

Notes: List of NCEs selected from Paul deHaen, Inc., *New Product Survey and Nonproprietary Name Index.* Codiscoverers are given one-half credit each; where the source could not be determined, it was assigned to "other."
Source: David Schwartzman, *Innovation in the Pharmaceutical Industry* (Baltimore: Johns Hopkins University Press, 1976), p. 74, and authors.

to 1975. U.S. firms discovered between 50 and 60 percent of the total (depending on which definition of country of origin is employed). Other major sources were the United Kingdom, Switzerland, West Germany, and Japan. The international character of the industry is also reflected in the multinational organizational structure of the major U.S. and foreign firms. The larger U.S. firms tend to have

TABLE 4

New Chemical Entities Introduced in the United States, by Country of Origin, 1963–1975

Country	NCEs Discovered[a]		NCEs Discovered[b]	
	Number	Percent	Number	Percent
United States	99.5	59	87.5	52
United Kingdom	18.5	11	22.5	13
Switzerland	9.5	6	18.5	11
West Germany	7.0	4	7.0	4
Japan	6.0	4	6.0	4
Others	28.5	17	27.5	16
Total	169	100	169	100

Note: Duplicate sources of discoveries are assigned a value of 0.5.

[a] Based on the country where the research and development were performed that first discovered the drug's pharmacological action.

[b] Based on the nationality of the parent firm sponsoring the research that first discovered the drug.

Source: Paul deHaen, Inc., various publications.

foreign research, production, and marketing subsidiaries, and many of the major foreign firms have similar facilities in the United States.

The drug discovery process is typically carried out by multidisciplinary research teams and is often characterized by lengthy trial-and-error search efforts. Serendipity has also been important in many major discoveries, the most famous example, of course, being Fleming's discovery of penicillin. The important major tranquilizer chlorpromazine was a result of the unexpected discovery that certain of the antihistamines are potent depressants of the central nervous system. Other examples include the antihypertensive actions of the β-blockers, the anti-inflammatory effects of the steroids, and the antigout action of allopurinol.

Random screening is another technique of drug discovery. Schwartzman has described one especially interesting example.[5] In search of a drug to combat tuberculosis, Lederle Laboratories systematically tested a file of 103,000 chemical compounds that had been developed by its parent company for a variety of purposes. After many years a compound originally developed for use as an antioxidant additive for rubber was found to be effective against tuberculosis. Six hundred similar compounds were synthesized, and the important antitubercular drug ethambutol was discovered.

These examples would suggest that drug discovery is largely a trial-and-error process. David Schwartzman has argued in favor of this view. He suggests that the majority of discoveries historically can be traced to one of three sources: naturally occurring compounds, accidental discoveries, and modification of previously known drugs. Nevertheless, even if this has traditionally been so, there appears to be a strong trend in recent years toward a more deductive, "discovery by design" approach in pharmaceutical industry laboratories.

According to William I. H. Shedden, vice-president in charge of clinical evaluation at Eli Lilly, scientists at Lilly are now taking a "very fundamental biological approach" in some of their research.[6] Shedden observes that in the old days the chemists would make a batch of compounds and send them over to the biologists to put into animals to see what would happen. Today the biologists ask the chemists to design molecules to accomplish particular effects.

A highly successful example of drug design is the antiulcer drug Tagamet. Knowing that the hormone histamine is a potent stimulant of the gastric secretions that can lead to ulcers, SmithKline scientists sought a compound that would inhibit the flow of histamine. They finally succeeded in designing a molecule that would lock onto a "receptor site," thereby blocking out the hormone and in turn the gastric secretions. In contrast to previous therapies, therefore, Tagamet allows ulcers to heal and frequently disappear rather than simply coating the stomach with antacids. It is an example of a pioneering drug that is likely to spawn a number of competitive therapies in the years ahead.

The increased propensity of firms toward an analytical discovery-by-design approach also points up the increasingly complementary relationship between private industry research and development (R and D) and more basic research in academic and government research laboratories. Biomedical research supported by the National Institutes of Health totaled approximately $3 billion in 1980. Findings from this research lead to a better understanding of the underlying causes of diseases and of how drug compounds interact with basic physiological properties. This has permitted firms increasingly to replace random screening with a targeted approach in which the molecules of a compound are designed in advance to accomplish a particular physiological response.

The R and D projects undertaken by the private pharmaceutical industry are thus related to and influenced by the basic biomedical research of the broader scientific community. There is a great deal of drug industry research on the body's immune response system and on enzyme chemistry and prostaglandins. The potential therapeutic applications are numerous, including more effective therapies for cardiovascular illnesses and cancer. Furthermore, recent advances in recombinant DNA, or "gene splicing," promise important application to future drug discovery and development. This new process has been used to induce bacteria to produce insulin and interferon and has exciting possibilities in several other areas. P. Roy Vagelos, head of research at Merck, has characterized current industry research possibilities as follows: "There has been a flowering of biomedical research. This is a fantastic time in biology. The companies with the right kind of people and resources can capitalize on it and bring the new knowledge to bear on the right diseases and compounds."[7]

Drug Development and the FDA's Role

The actual discovery of a new drug is only the first step in the lengthy process of drug innovation. In this section we turn to the development process for a drug candidate once it has been synthesized and initially screened in animal testing for potential therapeutic effects.

Figure 4, taken from an article by William M. Wardell, provides a good overview of the present system of drug development and FDA regulation.[8] Once a new chemical compound has been tested in animals

21

FIGURE 4
Drug Development in the United States

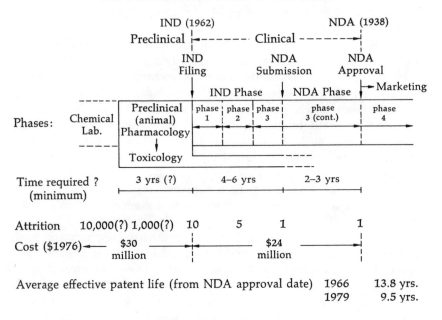

Source: Wardell, "History of Drug Discovery."

and found to be worthy of human testing, the developer must file an investigational new drug (IND) application with the FDA.

The FDA's decision to permit clinical testing is based on the following considerations: (1) the protection of the human research subject, (2) the adequacy of animal studies already completed, (3) the scientific merits of the research plan, and (4) the qualifications of the investigator.

If the FDA does not notify the developer within thirty days that clinical testing may not begin, the drug proceeds through three phases of clinical testing. The first phase, directed toward examining a drug's possible toxic effects, is performed on healthy individuals under highly controlled situations. If a drug successfully completes this stage, it is tested on a relatively small number of patients to examine its effectiveness. It is then carefully evaluated from a therapeutic and marketing standpoint before the decision to begin phase 3 is made. In phase 3 expanded studies are undertaken in large patient populations, with substantially greater expenditures. If a drug successfully passes these three phases of testing and is considered to have sufficient market value to warrant commercial introduction, a new drug application (NDA) is submitted to the FDA. Marketing can begin when approval of an NDA is received.

The NDA must include all the information the developer has obtained from tests of the safety and efficacy of the drug. It must also include information on how the drug is to be manufactured. An NDA consists of 2 to 15 volumes of summary material and 10 to 100 volumes of raw data.[9]

The FDA has 180 days in which to review the NDA and either approve or disapprove it. If the NDA is considered incomplete, the FDA can extend the period (with the applicant's permission) until further data are submitted.

The average time elapsed from NDA submission to final approval was fourteen months in 1963 and had increased to thirty-five months in 1979.[10] Later in this study we report the results of an analysis by the General Accounting Office (GAO) of the reasons for this lengthy review period.

The time required to pass through the three testing phases is shown in figure 4 as averaging four to six years, with an additional two to three years for NDA approval. The attrition rates show that for every ten drugs entering the IND stage, only one will have an NDA submission. Notice that figure 4 shows no further attrition. According to Wardell, "The one survivor that reaches an NDA submission has a ninety percent chance of being approved by the FDA, given five years for review at FDA."[11]

The cost figures shown in figure 4 are based on a study by Ronald W. Hansen.[12] Hansen obtained survey data from fourteen pharmaceutical firms on the R and D costs for a sample of NCEs first tested in human subjects from 1963 to 1975. The discovery cost per NCE was estimated at $30 million and the development cost at $24 million, for a total cost of $54 million. This $54 million is the capitalized value (at 8 percent interest and in 1976 dollars) at the date of marketing approval.

The $54 million includes the cost of NCEs that enter clinical testing but are not carried to the point of NDA approval. Hansen found, for example, that by the end of fifteen months of clinical testing, testing had ended on over 50 percent of the NCEs that had entered human trials. Hence the $54 million figure should be interpreted as the average expected cost of discovering and developing a marketable NCE.

The data in figure 4 on the expected patent life of a new drug indicate that the average effective life of an NCE has been declining and in 1979 was 9.5 years—about half the nominal life of 17 years.

TABLE 5

FDA Human Drugs Budget and Numbers
of New Drug Reviewers, by Specialty, 1966–1980

Year	Human Drugs Budget ($ millions)	Medical Officers	Chemists	Pharmacologists
1966	25.4	—	—	—
1967	28.9	—	—	—
1968	25.0	—	—	—
1969	29.5	—	—	—
1970	34.4	—	—	—
1971	44.3	80	51	47
1972	48.9	—	—	—
1973	57.7	76	45	35
1974	41.3	71	49	34
1975	45.9	74	56	41
1976	49.9	67	54	41
1977	59.5	76	56	41
1978	65.3	75	48	41
1979	68.9	74	47	40
1980	73.7	77	51	36

SOURCES: Budget figures taken from various Food and Drug Administration annual reports; numbers of new drug reviewers obtained from FDA, *New Drug Evaluation Project—Briefing Book*, March 1981.

This declining effective patent life is largely due to the longer development and regulatory approval times. This shortening patent life has become a major policy issue, which we discuss in chapter 4.

The Regulatory Process at the FDA

In the last section we discussed the role of the FDA largely from the perspective of the innovating firm. Here we turn to some specifics of the FDA and its procedures.

The FDA is part of the Public Health Service, which is located organizationally within the Department of Health and Human Services. Although the Bureau of Drugs is only one of a number of bureaus of the FDA, about 22 percent of the FDA's budget is allocated to its human drugs program, slightly less than the 27 percent allocated to food safety, its largest program.[13]

Table 5 shows the FDA's human drugs budget for the period 1966 to 1980 and the numbers of medical officers, chemists, and pharmacologists at the FDA who serve as reviewers of new drugs. The number of reviewers has remained about the same for the past ten years.

An innovating firm files an NDA with the FDA after completing the animal and clinical tests. All NDAs are reviewed by the Office of the Associate Director of New Drug Evaluation in the Bureau of Drugs. Six divisions within this office review NDAs, each being responsible for evaluating drugs in a particular therapeutic class or for use in a particular organ system.

The FDA uses a team approach to evaluating an NDA, as indicated in figure 5, which shows the path of an NDA through the FDA. The review team is made up of (1) a medical officer, who reviews the clinical test results; (2) a pharmacologist, who reviews the animal test results; and (3) a chemist, who reviews the chemistry and manufacturing controls and processes. The team may include additional specialists, such as a microbiologist or a statistician. It is coordinated by a supervisory medical officer.

Although figure 5 indicates that advisory committees are normally used in the review process, the FDA apparently relies less on such expert committees than regulatory authorities in other countries do. According to the 1980 GAO report that analyzed the FDA drug approval process:

> Some European committees of experts are mandated to review all drug applications and either approve a drug when it is shown to be safe and efficacious or recommend to the regulatory agency that a drug should or should not be approved. In three countries—the Netherlands, Norway, and Sweden—the committees had been given the responsibility to make the decision to approve, reject, or withdraw a drug. The United Kingdom's committee only advises the government agency on the safety and efficacy of a drug; however, we were told that its recommendations have always been followed.
>
> At FDA, committees are used to provide advice on problems or questions FDA may have concerning selected drug applications. However, applications are not submitted routinely to the committees in the United States as they are in foreign countries. FDA has sole responsibility for making a decision on an application based on the scientific data submitted and any advice from the expert committee.
>
> In most European countries we visited, all new drug applications are reviewed by expert committees, and the committees meet much more frequently than those in the

FIGURE 5
FDA Review Process for New Drug Applications

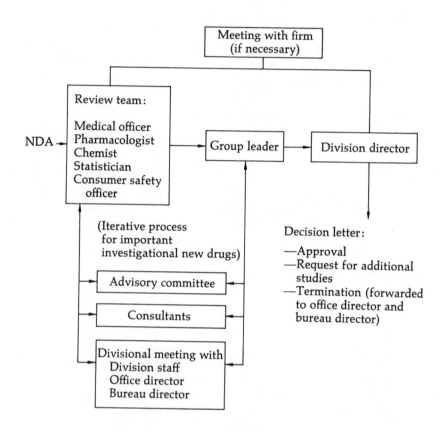

Source: House Subcommittee on Science, Research, and Technology, *Report on the Food and Drug Administration's Process for Approving New Drugs*, 1980, p. 18.

United States. In the United States, however, expert committees review only selected applications, and the committees meet at irregular intervals, some no more than twice a year. The long interval between meetings, according to one industry official, can delay the processing of NDA's.[14]

Another major difference between the United States and several advanced European countries lies in the extent of postmarketing surveillance. Many countries, such as the United Kingdom, have more intensive and stringent systems of postmarketing surveillance of NCEs than the United States. In part this reflects their more centralized national health delivery systems and a greater ability to gather more systematic data on a new drug's use by patients after it is introduced.

In any case, European countries tend to give more emphasis to postmarket surveillance in the regulatory process while the United States concentrates its regulatory efforts much more heavily on premarket controls. This is a basic difference in philosophy that is discussed further below.

Finally, we should note that the FDA has recently begun a program of "fast-tracking" certain NDAs through the review process. All drugs are now classified at a fairly early stage in the development process into three basic categories—drugs likely to be (1) an important advance, (2) a modest advance, or (3) little or no advance. The intention is to assign priorities for review in accordance with a drug's placement under this classification scheme. Although this approach may get some important therapies into public hands sooner, it is also subject to some possible problems. If the FDA's judgment on a new drug's therapeutic value is in error, it may delay rather than speed up the time for the drug to clear regulatory hurdles (that is, by putting an important drug on a slower track).

Notes

1. In preparing this chapter and the next, we have drawn heavily on our study "The Pharmaceutical Industry," in Richard R. Nelson, ed., *Government and Technical Progress: A Cross-Industry Analysis* (New York: Pergamon Press, 1982).

2. Victor R. Fuchs, *Who Shall Live?* (New York: Basic Books, 1974).

3. John F. Geweke and Burton A. Weisbrod, "Some Economic Consequences of Technological Advance in Medical Care: The Case of a New Drug," in Robert B. Helms, ed., *Drugs and Health* (Washington, D.C.: American Enterprise Institute, 1981).

4. Nelson S. Hartunian, Charles N. Smart, and Mark S. Thompson, "The Incidence and Economic Costs of Cancer, Motor Vehicle Injuries, Coronary Heart Disease, and Stroke: A Comparative Analysis," *American Journal of Public Health,* vol. 70 (1980), pp. 1249–60.

5. David Schwartzman, *Innovation in the Pharmaceutical Industry* (Baltimore: Johns Hopkins University Press, 1976).

6. See "Eli-Lilly: New Life in the Drug Industry," *Business Week,* October 29, 1979.

7. Ibid.

8. William M. Wardell, "The History of Drug Discovery, Development, and Regulation," in Robert I. Chien, ed., *Issues in Pharmaceutical Economics* (Lexington, Mass.: Lexington Books, 1979).

9. U.S. Congress, House, Subcommittee on Science, Research, and Technology of the Committee on Science and Technology, *Report on the Food and Drug Administration's Process for Approving New Drugs,* 96th Congress, 1st session, 1980, p. 17. One of the proposed regulatory changes of the Reagan administration is to reduce the amount of information required to be submitted in an NDA. See the discussion in chapter 5 on this point.

10. Ibid.

11. Wardell, "History of Drug Discovery," p. 10.

12. Ronald W. Hansen, "The Pharmaceutical Development Process: Estimates of Current Development Costs and Times and the Effects of Regulatory Changes," in Chien, *Issues in Pharmaceutical Economics.*

13. U.S. Food and Drug Administration, *Annual Report: 1979.*

14. U.S. General Accounting Office, *FDA Drug Approval—A Lengthy Process That Delays the Availability of Important New Drugs,* HRD-80-64, May 28, 1980, p. 34.

3

Trends in Drug Innovation and Empirical Studies of the Effects of Regulation

Since the early 1960s there have been a number of adverse trends in the innovative process in pharmaceuticals: a decline in the rate of new product introduction, higher costs, lengthier development periods. In this chapter we describe these trends and then examine various hypotheses that have been advanced to explain them. The effect of FDA regulation is, of course, a leading hypothesis, which was considered in some detail in chapter 1.

In the final section of this chapter, we consider some of the available evidence concerning the benefits of regulation. That is, to what extent has the United States gained from safer and more effective drugs as a result of FDA regulation?

Description of Adverse Trends

Figure 6 shows the annual number of new chemical entities (NCEs) introduced in the United States between 1954 and 1981. (New chemical entities are new compounds not previously marketed and include nearly all major therapeutic advances.) Also shown in figure 6 are the trends in NCEs discovered in the United States and total expenditures (in constant dollars) for research and development (R and D) by the domestic pharmaceutical industry.

The rate of introduction of NCEs has clearly declined since the late 1950s. From 1955 to 1960, for example, an average of about fifty NCEs per year were introduced. The corresponding number for the 1965–1970 period is only seventeen, and for the most recent six-year period the average is also seventeen.

This decline in new product introductions has been accompanied by corresponding structural trends on the input side of the innovational process. Given the increasing trend in R and D expenditures

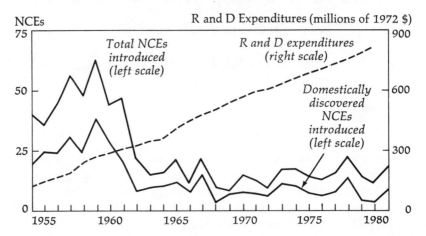

FIGURE 6

INTRODUCTION AND DISCOVERY OF NEW CHEMICAL ENTITIES BY
DOMESTIC FIRMS AND CONSTANT-DOLLAR EXPENDITURES ON
PHARMACEUTICAL RESEARCH AND DEVELOPMENT, 1954–1981

SOURCES: NCE introductions, Paul DeHaen, Inc., *New Drug Analysis USA*,
various issues; R and D expenditures, PMA *Annual Survey Reports*; for further
information see Grabowski, Vernon, and Thomas, "Estimating the Effects of
Regulation on Innovation," appendix.

shown in figure 6, it is evident that the R and D cost per NCE has been
rising. As discussed in chapter 2, Hansen estimated the cost in 1976
of developing an NCE at about $24 million. (This figure equals about
$16 million in uncapitalized 1976 dollars.) We may compare this
finding with those of prior studies by Clymer, Mund, and Sarett,
which put the uncapitalized development cost of an NCE in the range
of $1 million to $2 million in the early 1960s.[1] Moreover, Clymer
estimated that the attrition rate for drugs undergoing clinical tests
was two out of three before 1962. Current data analyzed by William
Wardell and reported in figure 4 suggest that only one in ten clinically
tested drug entities is introduced as a new drug. Finally, the average
gestation period for a successful new drug has also increased significantly, from four to six years in the early 1960s to ten years or more.

In table 6 we show R and D expenditures by the pharmaceutical
industry for the 1965–1980 period. The first column shows that
domestic R and D outlays in current dollars increased every year
during the period. When the R and D expenditures are adjusted
for inflation, the result is a growth rate of about 3 percent per year
in constant dollars over the last decade. We should note that the

TABLE 6

Domestic and Foreign Research and Development Expenditures of U.S. Ethical Drug Industry, 1965–1980

Year	Domestic R and D in Current Dollars (millions)	Domestic R and D in Constant Dollars[a] (millions)	Foreign R and D in Current Dollars (millions)	Ratio of Foreign R and D to Total R and D (percent)	Ratio of R and D to Sales[b] in Current Dollars (percent)
1965	304.1	304.1	24.5	7.5	8.3
1966	344.2	333.8	30.2	8.1	8.6
1967	377.9	355.4	34.5	8.4	8.7
1968	410.4	369.6	39.1	8.7	8.5
1969	464.1	397.6	41.7	8.2	8.7
1970	518.6	421.7	47.2	8.3	8.8
1971	576.5	446.5	52.3	8.3	8.6
1972	600.7	446.6	66.1	9.9	8.6
1973	643.8	452.9	108.7	14.4	8.6
1974	726.0	469.8	132.5	15.4	8.6
1975	828.6	490.7	144.9	14.9	8.4
1976	902.9	507.3	164.9	15.4	8.4
1977	984.1	522.5	197.7	16.7	8.5
1978	1,089.2	538.4	222.0	16.9	8.2
1979	1,243.1	565.6	279.8	18.4	8.3
1980	1,437.4[c]	598.3	337.2[c]	19.0	8.6

Note: For human-use pharmaceutical research and development; veterinary-use pharmaceutical R and D is excluded.

[a] Deflated by GNP price deflator converted to 1965 base.

[b] Global pharmaceutical R and D and sales of U.S. firms.

[c] Budgeted.

Sources: Pharmaceutical Manufacturers Association, *Factbook 1980* (Washington, D.C., 1980); and PMA, *1979–1980 Annual Survey Report of the U.S. Pharmaceutical Industry.*

GNP price deflator probably understates the true rate of price change; so the true growth rate may in fact be considerably smaller.

Table 6 also shows foreign research and development expenditures by U.S. firms for the period 1965–1980. Although it is not clear how to deflate these outlays, these data show that slower growth in domestic R and D has been offset in part by faster growth in foreign R and D expenditures. The proportion of total R and D accounted for by foreign R and D more than doubled, from 7.5 percent in 1965

31

FIGURE 7
INVESTIGATIONAL DRUGS BY U.S. FIRMS, 1958–1979

Number of investigational drugs

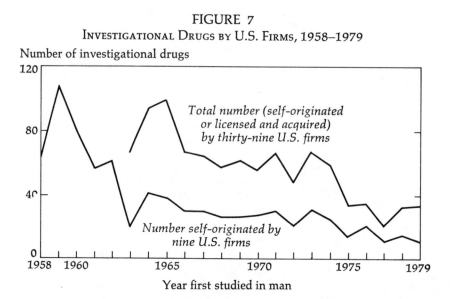

Year first studied in man

SOURCE: William Wardell and Lorraine Sheck, "Is Pharmaceutical Innovation Declining? Interpreting Measures of Pharmaceutical Innovation and Regulatory Impact in the USA, 1950–1980" (Paper presented to Arne Ryde Symposium on Pharmaceutical Innovation, Helsinborg, Sweden, September 28, 1982).

to 19 percent in 1980. This is consistent with the increasing trend in the percentage of revenues from foreign markets and also the possibility of incurring less stringent regulatory controls in early clinical trials abroad. It may, of course, reflect other economic factors as well.

The final column in table 6 gives the time trend in the ratio of global R and D expenditures to sales (including both domestic and foreign expenditures and sales) for U.S. firms. This ratio has been quite stable over the period, ranging between 8 and 9 percent.

The number of investigational drugs being studied in humans by U.S. firms has also significantly declined over time. Figure 7, based on data assembled by William Wardell on this issue, shows the number of self-originated investigational drugs by nine major U.S. research-intensive firms over the period 1958 to 1979 and the total number of investigational drugs by thirty-nine U.S. firms over the shorter period 1963 to 1979. Both curves show that there are far fewer drugs being clinically investigated by U.S. firms now than in earlier periods.

We consider finally what has been happening to the innovative structure of the pharmaceutical industry. Virts and Weston have

TABLE 7

Independent Firms Introducing New Chemical Entities in the U.S. Market, 1954–1980

Period	Number of Firms	Percent Foreign
1954–1958	51	14
1963–1967	41	17
1976–1980	36	31

Sources: John R. Virts and J. Fred Weston, "Returns to Research and Development in the U.S. Pharmaceutical Industry," *Managerial and Decision Economics* (September 1980). Data for 1976–1980 period obtained directly from authors.

examined the trend in the number of independent firms introducing at least one NCE. Their findings, reproduced in table 7, show that the number of such firms declined from fifty-one in the 1954–1958 period to forty-one in the 1963–1967 period and to thirty-six in the 1976–1980 period. While one might expect a decline in the number of firms achieving at least one NCE to parallel the decline in NCEs, it is nevertheless an indication that the number of independent sources of innovation is continuing to fall.

A further interesting result is the increasing percentage of these firms that are foreign owned. That percentage rose from 17 percent in the 1963–1967 period to 31 percent in the 1976–1980 period. One reason for the rise was the acquisition of domestic firms by foreign firms, but this is not a complete explanation. Further research is needed.

There thus has been a decline in annual new drug introductions accompanied by strong upward trends in the costs, times, and risks associated with discovering and developing new drugs. In economists' terminology, there has been a shift in the "production function" for new drug innovation in the direction of lower R and D productivity— that is to say, fewer new drug introductions are emanating from larger resource commitments by the industry.

The causes and importance of this decline in new drug introductions have roused considerable controversy, which has centered on the increased regulation resulting from the 1962 Kefauver-Harris amendments as a major cause of the decline in innovation. An initial response by the FDA was to argue that the observed decline in pharmaceutical innovation was in fact compositional rather than real:

The relevant question is not and never has been how many new drugs are marketed each year, but rather how many significant, useful, and unique therapeutic entities are developed. . . . The rate of development and marketing of truly important, significant, and unique therapeutic entities in this country has remained relatively stable for the past 22 years.[2]

It is difficult, however, to substantiate the FDA's claim that the observed decline in new drugs introduced has been largely confined to marginal drugs. It is true that the much higher costs and risks of developing new drugs have caused firms to focus less in their research programs on imitative drugs, which do appear to have declined disproportionately over time. Nevertheless, the evidence suggests a decline in therapeutically significant drugs as well. Most classifications of important therapeutic advances by academic analysts show such a decline, as does at least one prior FDA ranking of important drugs.[3]

Measures of pharmaceutical innovation based on economic criteria also suggest that a real decline has occurred. If we examine a market share measure that indicates the relative importance of NCE sales in total ethical drug sales, we find that the share of NCEs fell from 20 percent in 1957–1961 to 8.6 percent in 1962–1966 and to 6.2 percent in 1972–1976.[4] Of course, these economic measures tend to give little weight to major therapeutic advances for relatively rare diseases. It is unlikely, however, that the downward trend can be primarily explained by an increasing proportion of such innovations, given the adverse economic shifts in the costs of discovering and developing new drugs that occurred in this period.

Sam Peltzman has analyzed a related drug quality issue: whether the large decline in NCEs introduced can be explained by the entry of fewer ineffective drugs after the 1962 amendments were passed.[5] His analysis of data from three groups of experts—hospitals, panels employed by state public assistance agencies, and the American Medical Association's Council on Drugs—does not support this view. These data suggest that only a small fraction of the NCEs introduced before 1962 could be classified as ineffective.

In sum, the hypothesis that the observed decline in new product introductions has largely been concentrated in marginal or ineffective drugs is not generally supported by empirical analyses. If one accepts that a significant decline in drug innovation occurred in the 1960s and 1970s, the question of the role of regulatory and nonregulatory factors in explaining this decline remains. In the remainder of this section we consider various possible answers to this question and the evidence from various analyses of the issue.

Alternative Hypotheses for Explaining Adverse Trends

Increased Regulation. A major legislative change occurred in 1962 with the passage of the Kefauver-Harris amendments to the Food, Drug, and Cosmetic Act. Two basic provisions of these amendments directly affected the drug innovation process: (1) the proof-of-efficacy requirement for new drug approval and (2) the establishment of FDA regulatory controls over the clinical (human) testing of new drug candidates. In addition, the attention of Congress and the media to new drug approvals increased dramatically after 1962. This increased attention intensified the pressures to avoid type 2 errors (allowing a risky drug into the marketplace) at the expense of type 1 errors (rejection or delays in the introduction of a beneficial drug).

In sum, there was a substantial increase in both the scope and the intensity of regulatory controls on ethical drugs after 1962. As a consequence, it has been postulated that the cost of discovering and developing a new drug, along with the risk and uncertainty of drug innovation, has increased and that this has been a major cause of the observed decline in new drug innovation in the United States.

Depletion of Research Opportunities. The research depletion hypothesis has been given the most attention in the literature as an alternative to increased regulation. Adherents of the hypothesis argue that major drug innovations tend to occur in waves or cycles and that in many major therapeutic areas we have reached a point where the probability that a new discovery will be an advance over existing therapies is quite low. They further argue that we are on a research plateau because the major disease areas left to conquer are those in which we have the least adequate scientific understanding of the underlying biological processes. As former FDA Commissioner Schmidt has argued:

> As the gaps in biomedical knowledge decrease, so do the opportunities for the development of new or useful related drugs. As shown by the declining number of new single entity drugs approved in the U.S., England, France and Germany, this is an international phenomenon. This does not reflect a loss of innovative capacity, but rather reflects the normal course of a growth industry as it becomes technologically more mature.[6]

This hypothesis, advanced by the FDA and others, has been received with considerable skepticism in many scientific quarters. Some have challenged the hypothesis on conceptual grounds. Others have pointed to the vast expenditures on basic biomedical research by the National Institutes of Health and other organizations as creating a renewed pool of basic knowledge that should offset any tendency toward a depletion of opportunities from prior drug discoveries. The evidence on this issue from international data on introductions, referred to by FDA Commissioner Schmidt, is discussed in detail below.

Changing Expectations. In addition to increased regulation and research depletion, Lebergott has pointed to the effects of the thalidomide tragedy on the behavior and expectations of physicians and drug firms as further confounding factors. He argues:

> Do any of us believe that after that catastrophe, consumers were quite as likely as before to prefer new drugs to ones tested by experience? Were physicians henceforth quite as likely to prescribe new drugs—with the prospect of acute toxicity (and malpractice suits) when the one chance of 10,000 ran against them? Which of our leading pharmaceutical firms would henceforth endanger its reputation (and its entire existing product line) on behalf of a new drug on quite the same terms as it did in the days when biochemists could do no wrong? . . . Such massive changes in the U.S. perspective on drugs—we may call them shifts in both supply and demand curves—had to cut the number of more venturesome drugs put under investigation since 1962. It would have done so if the entire FDA staff had gone fishing for the next couple of years.[7]

Lebergott argues, then, that strong shifts in the incentive structure facing physicians and manufacturers occurred after thalidomide and that these would independently operate to increase R and D costs and decrease new drug introductions. His analysis points up the analytical difficulties in trying to identify the effects of regulatory and nonregulatory factors that changed simultaneously as a result of the thalidomide incident.

Advances in Pharmacological Science. Pettinga and others have pointed to scientific advances in pharmacological science over the past few decades as another potentially important factor.[8] Pettinga suggests that these advances, which have made teratological and toxicological studies much more sophisticated and costly, would have been incorporated into drug firms' testing procedures even in the absence of regulatory requirements. That is, drug firms would undertake many of these tests in their own self-interest, to reduce the likelihood of future losses in good-will and potential legal liabilities.

Several plausible hypotheses have thus been advanced to explain the observed downward trend in drug innovation. These hypotheses are not mutually exclusive and may all have contributed significantly to declining innovation in ethical drugs. In the next sections, we discuss the empirical evidence concerning the relative importance of increased government regulation and of these alternative explanations of declining drug innovation.

Studies of Regulatory Effects on Drug Innovation

Economic Analyses of Peltzman and Baily. Sam Peltzman's study of the effect of the 1962 amendments has received considerable attention from both economists and policy makers.[9] Peltzman employs a "demand pull" model in which the supply of new drugs in any period responds with a lag to shifts in demand-side factors. The model is estimated on preamendment data (1948–1962) and then employed to forecast what the number of NCEs would have been in the post-1962 period in the absence of regulation. The effects of the 1962 amendments are computed as the residual difference between the predicted and the actual flows of NCEs. Peltzman concludes that "all the difference between the pre-1962 and post-1962 new chemical entity flow can be attributed to the 1962 amendments." His approach, however, never formally includes or considers any of the supply-side factors in the hypotheses cited above. All the observed residual difference after 1962 is attributed to increased regulation. Since this residual difference can plausibly reflect a number of the other factors cited (research depletion, changing expectations, and scientific factors), it probably encompasses various nonregulatory phenomena as well.

Martin Baily employed a production function model of drug development, which does try explicitly to separate the effects of regulation from the depletion of scientific opportunities.[10] He postulates that the number of new chemical entities introduced in any period will be a function of lagged industry R and D expenditures and that both regulation and research depletion effects operate to shift this R and D production function over time. Regulation is captured explicitly in Baily's model by a time intercept shift variable and depletion by a moving average of past introductions. Both variables were quantitatively and statistically significant when his model was estimated over the period 1954 to 1969. When the model was later estimated for the period extending through 1974, however, the research depletion variable became insignificant and unstable over time.

Thus the early time series studies of this issue by Peltzman and Baily both found strong negative effects of regulation on new drug innovation. Neither study offered a very satisfactory way to isolate the effects of regulation from other confounding effects. This is a difficult econometric problem to handle in the context of aggregate time series analysis of U.S. introductions.

International Drug Lag Analysis by Wardell and Others. To separate the effects of increased regulation from other hypothesized factors, one would ideally perform an "experiment" involving two different states of the world: one with the 1962 amendments in effect and one without. Given the impossibility of this experiment, a second-best analysis may be to find another country as similar to the United States as possible that differs significantly in regulatory controls and procedures.

With this kind of methodological approach in mind, William Wardell, a clinical pharmacologist, performed a series of comparative analyses of drug introductions in the United States and the United Kingdom in the post-1962 period. The United Kingdom is similar to the United States in high standards of medical training and practice and also has a very research-intensive, multinational drug industry. The regulatory systems in effect in the United Kingdom and the United States in the post-1962 period have important differences. Premarket safety reviews of new drugs essentially began in 1963 in the United Kingdom as a response to the thalidomide tragedy. Those reviews have been characterized as of high quality in the depth of the review process and the type of evidence necessary to gain approval. The United Kingdom did not require formal proof of efficacy until its Medicine Act was implemented in 1971; before that date the task of evaluating a drug's efficacy was essentially left to the market mechanism. Further, the British investigational new drug procedure was voluntary until 1971. Moreover, the British system uses the judgment of external committees of academic medical experts in deciding whether to approve new drugs and emphasizes postmarket surveillance to a much greater degree than the U.S. system. As a result, the British system has been characterized as less adversarial and bureaucratic than the U.S. system, which relies to a greater extent on the decisions of career civil servants, congressional oversight hearings, and the judicial process.

Wardell's first comparative study of new drug introductions in the United States and the United Kingdom covered nine therapeutic classes for the period 1962–1971.[11] For this period the number of new chemical entities introduced in the United Kingdom (159) was roughly 50 percent higher than the number introduced in the United

States (103). Moreover, of the drugs that were available in both countries by 1971, twice as many were introduced first in the United Kingdom as were introduced first in the United States. This "drug lag" was found to be greatest in the areas of cardiovascular, diuretic, gastrointestinal, and respiratory medicine. In cancer chemotherapy, Wardell found that new therapies were comparably available in both countries.

In a follow-up to his original drug lag study, Wardell found comparable trends for the 1972–1976 period in the aggregate numbers of exclusive introductions and comparable lags in mutually available drugs.[12] He also noted some tendency for the largest clinical differences to narrow over time. He attributed this convergence in part to more "realistic" regulatory standards in the United States in some areas and a trend to more conservative practices abroad.

In another paper Grabowski analyzes the time pattern of all NCE introductions in the United States for the period 1963 to 1975 in relation to the patterns in three European countries—the United Kingdom, Germany, and France.[13] He finds that NCE introductions in the United States have lagged significantly behind those in the United Kingdom and Germany since 1962. This is true both for NCEs discovered in this country and for those discovered abroad. The United States still generally leads France in the introduction of U.S.-discovered NCEs but not of foreign-discovered ones. His analysis also indicates that the lag behind Europe is not confined to drugs with little or modest medical gain but includes drugs classified as significant therapeutic advances by the FDA itself. Further, a regression analysis performed in the paper provides evidence that lags in regulatory approval have contributed significantly to the lag in introductions. Finally, the analysis indicates that regulation has had an especially strong effect on the introduction lag for foreign-discovered drugs.

A recently released GAO study of the FDA drug approval process also examined the availability of fourteen therapeutically important drugs in the United States and five other countries (Canada, Norway, Sweden, Switzerland, and the United Kingdom).[14] This study focuses on drugs introduced in the United States between 1975 and 1978. As shown in table 8, it found that all but one of these fourteen drugs were available first abroad from two months to thirteen years before they were introduced in the United States. Furthermore, it found that the average FDA approval time of twenty-three months for these drugs was significantly greater than for all other countries except Sweden (England and Switzerland having average regulatory approval times of five and twelve months respectively).

TABLE 8

Date of Availability of Fourteen Therapeutically Important Drugs
(earliest date in italics)

Drug	United States	Canada	Norway	Sweden	Switzer- land	United Kingdom
Beclomethasone dipropionate	May 1976	June 1976	Nov. 1973	Mar. 1974	Nov. 1973	*Oct. 1972*
Sodium valproate	Feb. 1978	(a)	(b)	(a)	*May 1972*	Aug. 1972
Cimetidine	Aug. 1977	May 1977	July 1978	June 1978	Sept. 1977	Nov. 1976
Protirelin	Nov. 1976	(a)	(b)	Dec. 1976	Jan. 1977	*Jan. 1975*
Vidabrine	Nov. 1976	*Aug. 1976*	(b)	(c)	(c)	July 1977
Somatotropin	July 1976	(a)	(b)	*May 1971*	Apr. 1972	Feb. 1972
Sodium iodide I-123	Mar. 1976	(d)	(b)	(c)	(c)	(c)

Diazoxide	May 1976	July 1969	Dec. 1975	(a)	Dec. 1973	(c)
Phospho lipids	Oct. 1975	Oct. 1972	(b)	Feb. 1964	Jan. 1963	Jan. 1975
Amino acids	Dec. 1975	May 1977	(b)	Nov. 1972	Feb. 1966	(c)
Danazol	June 1976	Jan. 1976	May 1978	Oct. 1977	Apr. 1977	June 1974
Prazosin	June 1976	Aug. 1976	Sept. 1976	(a)	June 1974	Oct. 1973
Disopyramide phosphate	Aug. 1977	Mar. 1977	Aug. 1978	May 1978	Mar. 1977	July 1972
Propranolol:						
Arrhythmias	Nov. 1967	July 1968	Sept. 1966	Nov. 1965	Oct. 1965	June 1965
Angina	Nov. 1967	June 1969	Sept. 1966	Nov. 1965	Oct. 1965	June 1965
Hypertension	June 1976	July 1974	Aug. 1972	Nov. 1965	Oct. 1965	Apr. 1969

a Under review by agency at completion of our visit.
b Not submitted to agency at completion of our visit.
c Data not available.
d NDA submission canceled.

Source: U.S. General Accounting Office, FDA Drug Approval—A Lengthy Process That Delays the Availability of Important New Drugs, HRD-80-64, May 28, 1980, p. 68.

Some Additional Studies of Regulatory Effects

While a pattern of lagging U.S. introduction of NCEs (including therapeutically important drugs) thus emerges from a number of recent studies, a broader issue is the effect of regulation on the number, rather than the timing, of introductions. This may be characterized as the issue of drug loss rather than drug lag. It is the issue addressed by the earlier econometric analyses of Peltzman and Baily. As noted above, however, these aggregate time series studies had substantial difficulties in separating the effects of regulation from such other confounding factors as research depletion.

One may, of course, view the drug lag findings as symptomatic of broader effects of regulation on the innovation process—that is, regulation leading to greater costs, development times, and commercial uncertainties for new drugs and hence to fewer annual NCEs developed and introduced each year. The magnitude of these effects is arguable and remains an important issue for empirical research.

In a study that the authors performed jointly with Lacy Thomas, we examined aggregate R and D productivity changes in the United States and the United Kingdom to gain some insight into the effects of regulation on innovation.[15] Our strategy was to structure the analysis in terms of an econometric model and to use international data as a means of separating regulatory from nonregulatory factors. We found in this analysis that R and D productivity in the United States—defined as the number of new chemical entities discovered and introduced in the United States per dollar of R and D expenditure—declined about sixfold between 1960–1961 and 1966–1970. The corresponding decrease of R and D productivity in the United Kingdom was about threefold. From a regression analysis using these and other data, we concluded that increased regulation since 1962 has probably at least, doubled the cost of obtaining an NCE. At the same time, nonregulatory factors (such as research depletion, scientific advances in detecting toxicology, changing expectations) apparently have also significantly increased costs here and in the United Kingdom. The specific mechanisms and magnitudes of these different regulatory and nonregulatory factors await a more extensive and detailed analysis.

A recent economic study of regulatory effects by Steven Wiggins is performed on more disaggregate data than the prior literature.[16] Wiggins analyzes data on R and D expenditures and NCEs introduced by individual therapeutic class (for example, anti-infectives, cardiovasculars) over the period 1970 through 1976. His measure of regulatory stringency is based on NDA approval times, and he controls for differences in research opportunities through therapeutic class intercept dummy variables. His results imply a strong negative effect of regulation on the number of NCEs introduced. He estimates that regulation has decreased the number of introductions by 40 percent from what it would otherwise have been. This estimated effect is due both to a significant negative effect of regulation on R and D productivity and to an induced decline in the R and D expenditures that would have occurred in the absence of increased regulation. The magnitudes observed are roughly consistent with those found in our more aggregate international comparative analysis involving much longer time periods. Both types of studies indicate that increased regulation has been one of the primary causes of declining innovation.

Evidence of Improved Safety and Efficacy of New Drugs Due to Regulation

In chapter 1 we described the problem of regulation as one of balancing the costs of drug lag and drug loss against the benefits of safer and more effective drugs. In figure 2 we indicated that as the level of premarket testing increases, the expected health costs from the use of drugs that are not safe and effective should fall. The assumption, of course, is that the FDA has increased premarket testing above the level that would prevail if the FDA did not exist. In this section we turn to the question of the magnitude of the reduced drug toxicity resulting from this increased premarket testing.

Obviously, estimation of these benefits is difficult. It is of the same order of difficulty as estimating drug loss. The problem is basically to estimate the harm that never occurred because the FDA screened out unsafe or ineffective drugs that would have been marketed. Nevertheless, some studies have attempted such estimates, and we describe their results here.

Peltzman's study attempted to quantify the benefits to consumers from the efficacy provision of the 1962 Kefauver-Harris amendments.[17] He viewed the benefits as the saving of expenditures that consumers would otherwise have wasted on ineffective drugs. Peltzman estimated econometrically a demand schedule for new drugs from data on drug output and prices (aggregated by therapeutic class) in the periods before and after the amendments. He concluded that the reduced waste on purchases of ineffective new drugs was smaller (under $100 million) than the drug loss cost ($300–400 million), which he also estimated.

Peltzman's analysis can be criticized on several levels. His use of consumer surplus methodology is questionable in markets like drugs where consumers have a limited role in selecting the final products consumed. In addition, McGuire, Nelson, and Spavins have pointed out some technical problems in using aggregate demand curves to deduce how individual consumers learn and respond to uncertainties about drug efficacy.[18]

In addition to the econometric analysis, Peltzman analyzed evaluations by three groups of experts of drug efficacy before and after the 1962 amendments were passed. The question was whether these experts found the incidence of ineffective new drugs lower in the post-amendment period. Peltzman's conclusion was that the fraction of new drugs that are ineffective was about the same in the two periods, which supports his earlier conclusion of relatively small benefits.

An alternative approach is to use international comparative analysis. We described this method in our discussion of the Wardell analyses of drug lag. In short, the idea is to examine the health costs experienced in other countries in which regulatory controls are less restrictive than FDA controls.

In testimony before the House Committee on Science and Technology in 1979, Wardell described drugs that had been introduced in Europe and withdrawn after toxic effects were discovered. These drugs are listed in table 9. None were approved for marketing in the United States.

One of these drugs, practolol, has received especially great attention as an example of the benefits of FDA regulation. Barbara Moulton, a former FDA employee who testified before the same congressional committee, reported that practolol had been withdrawn from general use in Britain because it had been found to damage eyesight in some patients. It also induced the growth of a strangulating membrane in the bowels of others, some of whom died undergoing remedial surgery. According to Moulton's testimony, the most serious problem—permanent or near-permanent blindness—affected about one in 12,500 people for whom the drug was prescribed.[19]

Wardell's interpretation of the practolol episode is as follows:

> Most of the arguments that seek to deny the drug lag problems are based on the allegation that the new-drug toxicity that the U.S. has avoided by the drug lag is of very large size; there has even been a claim of benefit to the United States in the form of a "death lag." It is ironic that practolol, the drug chosen to illustrate this connection, has, despite its known toxicity, an extremely high benefit-to-risk ratio when used to prevent heart attacks and coronary death. If it were

TABLE 9
Drugs Removed from the European Market, 1964–1975

Drug	Use	Major Adverse Reaction
Practolol (United Kingdom, 1969)	Antihypertensive	Severe conjunctivitis (withdrawn, 1975)
Medihaler–Iso Forte (stronger form of isoprotarenol than approved in the United States)	Antiasthmatic	Deaths (withdrawn)
Aminorex (Switzerland, 1965)	Appetite suppressant	Pulmonary hypertension (withdrawn, 1968)
Ibufenac (United Kingdom, 1966)	Analgesic, anti-inflammatory	Jaundice, hepatotoxicity (withdrawn, 1968)
Benziodarone	Antiangina	Jaundice (withdrawn, 1964)

Source: U.S. Congress, House, Subcommittee on Science, Research, and Technology of the Committee on Science and Technology, *Report on the Food and Drug Administration's Process for Approving New Drugs,* 96th Congress, 1st session, 1980, p. 32.

available and used optimally in post-myocardial infarct patients in the U.S., this drug could be saving 10,000 to 20,000 lives a year, with a degree of toxicity that would now be small and controllable, and highly acceptable compared with the lifesaving benefit provided. To call the practolol example a "death lag" is a cynical inversion of the facts.[20]

Wardell summarized his analysis of the benefits of FDA regulation as follows: "The answer to the question 'has the United States saved some toxicity by a conservative posture?' is 'Yes.' But, I would contend that this saving has been very small compared with the benefits forgone."[21]

In a 1980 report on the FDA's process for approving new drugs, the House Subcommittee on Science, Research, and Technology of the Committee on Science and Technology commented that "the United States was apparently spared some toxicity problems which developed in Europe simply through FDA's routine administration process, during which time the adverse effects of drugs already on the market in Europe became apparent."[22] According to the report, U.S. non-approval was based on European experience rather than on information gained through premarket testing.

In 1982 the antiarthritic drug Oraflex was withdrawn from the United States a few months after its introduction. This occurred when the drug was suspended in Great Britain because of reported illnesses and deaths among elderly patients. This is an example of an earlier drug introduction abroad that provided the U.S. authorities with information on side effects from large patient populations much sooner than if the United States had been the initial adopter of the drug.

Summary and Conclusions

The United States has clearly realized some benefits from its very conservative approach to drug regulation compared with other countries. Our analysis in chapter 1 argued, however, that there are strong incentives in our system for the FDA to err on the side of too much delay and to be overrestrictive in approvals (that is, to avoid type 2 errors at the expense of type 1 errors). The empirical studies considered in this chapter are generally consistent with this point of view. There is evidence from several independent academic studies, using different methodological approaches, that increased FDA regulation has had significant adverse effects on the amounts of R and D and innovation during the 1960s and 1970s. In addition, the international comparative studies indicate that U.S. citizens have experienced sizable forgone health benefits from regulatory-induced delays

in obtaining beneficial new drugs while obtaining relatively modest
benefits in the form of less exposure to drug toxicity.

Notes

1. Harold A. Clymer, "The Changing Costs and Risks of Pharmaceutical
Innovation," in Joseph D. Cooper, ed., *The Economics of Drug Innovation*
(Washington, D.C.: American University, 1970); Vernon A. Mund, "The
Return on Investment of the Innovative Pharmaceutical Firm," in Cooper,
Economics of Drug Innovation; and Lewis H. Sarett, "FDA Regulations and
Their Influence on Future R & D," *Research Management* (March 1974).

2. Alexander Schmidt, "The FDA Today: Critics, Congress, and Consumerism," speech delivered before the National Press Club, Washington,
D.C., October 29, 1974.

3. See Henry G. Grabowski, *Drug Regulation and Innovation: Empirical
Evidence and Policy Options* (Washington, D.C.: American Enterprise
Institute, 1976), especially table 2.

4. The market share equals the average annual sales of all NCEs introduced during the period as a percentage of total ethical drug sales in the
last year of the period. The analysis is explained in more detail in Henry G.
Grabowski and John M Vernon, "Structural Effects of Regulation on Innovation in the Ethical Drug Industry," in Robert T. Masson and P. David
Qualls, eds., *Essays on Industrial Organization in Honor of Joe S. Bain*
(Cambridge, Mass.: Ballinger, 1976).

5. Sam Peltzman, *Regulation of Pharmaceutical Innovation: The 1962
Amendments* (Washington, D.C.: American Enterprise Institute, 1974).

6. U.S. Congress, House, Subcommittee on Health of the Committee
on Labor and Public Welfare, "Examination of the Pharmaceutical Industry,
1973–74, Part 1: Hearings on S.3441 and S.966," statement by Alexander
Schmidt, 93d Congress, 2d session, 1974, p. 272.

7. U.S. Congress, House, Subcommittee on Monopoly of the Select
Committee on Small Business, "Competitive Problems in the Drug Industry,
Part 23: Development and Marketing of Prescription Drugs," statement by
Stanley Lebergott, 93d Congress, 1st session, 1973, p. 9843.

8. Neil Pettinga, "Discussion," in Joseph D. Cooper, ed., *Regulation,
Economics, and Pharmaceutical Innovation* (Washington, D.C.: American
University, 1976).

9. Peltzman, *Regulation of Pharmaceutical Innovation.*

10. Martin N. Baily, "Research and Development Costs and Returns:
The U.S. Pharmaceutical Industry," *Journal of Political Economy* (January/
February 1972).

11. William M. Wardell, "Introduction of New Therapeutic Drugs in the
United States and Great Britain: An International Comparison," *Clinical
Pharmacology and Therapeutics* (September/October 1973).

12. William M. Wardell et al., "The Rate of Development of New Drugs
in the United States," *Clinical Pharmacology and Therapeutics* (May 1978).

13. Henry G. Grabowski, "Regulation and the International Diffusion of Pharmaceuticals," in Robert B. Helms, ed., *The International Supply of Medicines* (Washington, D.C.: American Enterprise Institute, 1980).

14. U.S. General Accounting Office, *FDA Drug Approval—A Lengthy Process That Delays the Availability of Important New Drugs*, HRD-80-64, May 28, 1980.

15. Henry G. Grabowski, John M. Vernon, and Lacy G. Thomas, "Estimating the Effects of Regulation on Innovation: An International Comparative Analysis of the Pharmaceutical Industry," *Journal of Law and Economics* (April 1978).

16. Steven Wiggins, "Product Quality Regulation and Innovation in the Pharmaceutical Industry," *Review of Economics and Statistics* (November 1981).

17. Peltzman, *Regulation of Pharmaceutical Innovation*.

18. Thomas McGuire, Richard Nelson, and Thomas Spavins, "An Evaluation of Consumer Protection Legislation: The 1962 Drug Amendments, A Comment," *Journal of Political Economy* (May/June 1975).

19. U.S. Congress, House, Subcommittee on Science, Research, and Technology of the Committee on Science and Technology, statement by Barbara Moulton, 96th Congress, 1st session, July 1979, p. 402.

20. U.S. Congress, House, Subcommittee on Science, Research, and Technology of the Committee on Science and Technology, *Report on The Food and Drug Administration's Process for Approving New Drugs*, 96th Congress, 1st session, 1980, p. 32.

21. U.S. Congress, House, Subcommittee on Science, Research, and Technology of the Committee on Science and Technology, statement by William M. Wardell, 96th Congress, 1st session, June 1979, p. 83.

22. House, Subcommittee on Science, Research, and Technology, *Food and Drug Administration's Process*, p. 33.

4

The Relation of FDA Regulation to Other Government Policies

FDA regulation is only one of several government policies affecting pharmaceutical innovation. These policies are often interdependent in their influence on the incentives for innovation.

An indirect but significant effect of regulation has been a reduction in the effective patent life of a new drug. This reduction has occurred because the average time required to develop a new chemical entity (NCE) and gain regulatory approval far exceeds the time needed to obtain a patent. Table 10 shows the trend in average effective patent lives of NCEs over the period 1966 to 1979. As the investigational new drug (IND) period and the new drug application (NDA) approval times have lengthened, the average effective patent life has correspondingly declined. It is now less than ten years.

This decline in effective patent life assumes potentially increased importance because of other institutional changes now taking place, specifically the repeal of state antisubstitution laws and the growth of the maximum allowable cost program and other government reimbursement cost control programs. The state antisubstitution laws, enacted in the 1950s, prohibited pharmacists from substituting any product for the specific brand written on the prescription. These laws often made it possible for innovators' products, through strong loyalties built up during the period of exclusivity, to maintain dominant market positions even after patents expired. Even after low-cost generic products became available when patents expired, physicians often continued to prescribe the brand name product, and pharmacists were required to dispense it.

A major structural change occurring in recent years has been the replacement of antisubstitution laws with product selection laws. All but a few states now permit some form of substitution by pharmacists. The individual state laws have significant differences, but essentially all enable pharmacists to substitute generic products (some mandate substitution) unless a physician prevents substitution by

TABLE 10
Average Effective Patent Life of New Chemical Entities Introduced in the United States, 1966–1979
(years)

Year	Average Effective Patent Life	Year	Average Effective Patent Life
1966	13.6	1973	12.1
1967	14.4	1974	13.0
1968	13.5	1975	11.4
1969	12.7	1976	11.3
1970	14.4	1977	9.6
1971	12.2	1978	10.5
1972	10.9	1979	9.5

NOTE: Effective patent life is the length of time from the date of FDA approval until the date of patent expiration.

SOURCE: Computed by University of Rochester Center for the Study of Drug Development; for a further discussion of these data, see Martin M. Eisman and William Wardell, "The Decline in Effective Patent Life of New Drugs," *Research Management* (January 1981), pp. 18-21.

checking a preprinted box or by writing "dispense as written" or "medically necessary" on the prescription form.[1] If substitution laws foster increased competition for the innovator's product, the length of patent protection will obviously have a much more critical effect on innovators' revenues.

Our main objective in this chapter is to investigate the significance of the interdependencies among government regulatory, patent, product selection, and cost reimbursement policies. In contrast to the historically based analyses discussed in chapter 3, our analysis here is oriented more to the future. We wish to gain insight into how increased competition from generics and imitative products in the future is likely to affect the expected profitability of R and D investment. We also want to examine how changes in various government policies might influence this situation.

We recently performed a sensitivity analysis on the expected profitability of pharmaceutical R and D investment.[2] We examined the effect on profitability of changes in such factors as the legal patent life, different degrees of expected product substitution, and changes in R and D costs associated with shorter regulatory approval times. The objective of our analysis was to gauge the economic significance for R and D profitability of various emerging trends and possible policy changes that are now being discussed and could soon occur.

The baseline for our study is the estimated distribution of returns for all U.S.-discovered introductions from 1970 to 1976. This is the most current sample period for which sufficiently lengthy time series data could be assembled to form reliable estimates of profitability. The characteristics of these baseline estimates are discussed first, and the findings of the sensitivity analysis follow. The final section discusses the implications of our results for policy.

Estimated Returns on NCE Introductions in the 1970s

Our baseline sample consists of thirty-seven NCEs discovered and introduced in the United States from 1970 to 1976. These span a broad range of therapeutic classes. Audit data on U.S. sales revenue and promotion costs were obtained for each of these drugs from the year of introduction through 1980. Average R and D costs were then estimated by therapeutic class.

The R and D estimates are based on a study by Hansen. Hansen obtained survey data from fourteen pharmaceutical firms on the R and D costs for a sample of NCEs first tested in human subjects from 1963 to 1975. The average discovery cost was $19.6 million, and the average development cost was $14.1 million, for a total of $33.7 million. The $33.7 million is the capitalized value (at 10 percent interest and in 1967 dollars) at the date of marketing approval.

At our request Hansen estimated the costs per NCE by therapeutic class.[3] These are the cost estimates used in this analysis; as we will show, they reveal a rather large variation across classes. We should also note that Hansen's estimates include the costs of NCEs that enter clinical testing but are not carried to the point of NDA approval. Hence the estimates should be interpreted as the average expected cost of discovering and developing a marketable NCE.

Some general information about the R and D cost estimate is presented in table 11. What is particularly striking is the relatively low estimate of the expected present value of R and D costs for a new chemical entity in anti-infectives ($19.1 million) compared with therapeutic classes such as psychopharmacology ($70.0 million), metabolic-antifertility ($65.3 million), and anti-inflammatory ($68.3 million). This is consistent with a significant regulatory effect on the cost of developing new entities since anti-infectives are the easiest drugs for which to establish efficacy using the "large and well-controlled trials" criterion of the FDA.

Hansen's estimates are expressed as capitalized values at the date

TABLE 11

RESEARCH AND DEVELOPMENT COSTS FOR SAMPLE OF THIRTY-SEVEN NCEs USED IN SENSITIVITY ANALYSIS

Therapeutic Class	Hansen's R and D Cost (10 percent, 1967 $ million)	Number of U.S. NCEs
Cardiovascular	30.6	4
Neurologic, analgesic	36.3	6
Psychopharmacological	70.0	3
Metabolic, antifertility	65.3	5
Anti-infective	19.1	12
Anti-inflammatory	68.3	4
Gastrointestinal, respiratory, surgical	28.5	3

of marketing. The capitalized expected cost of discovering and developing a cardiovascular drug, for example, at the date of marketing is $30.6 million in 1967 dollars. Because he worked with constant dollars, Hansen used real interest rates; in the example above, the interest rate is 10 percent. The natural returns measure for comparison with Hansen's cost estimate is the present value of the net revenue stream resulting from the NCE (that is, after subtracting the costs of production, promotion, administration). To be consistent, of course, the net revenue stream must be deflated to 1967 dollars and discounted to the date of marketing at the same real interest rate. This was done in our analysis. Two additional important types of data were not available: the cost of producing the NCEs after FDA approval and the net revenues resulting from sales in foreign countries. In both cases we have relied on estimates made by Celia Thomas as part of her Ph.D. dissertation at Duke University.[4] Her best estimate for production and administration costs as a fraction of sales is 0.30. Because of uncertainty about this estimate, we also examined the effect of estimates of 0.20 and 0.40. We took a similar approach to Thomas's estimate of 1.75 as the ratio of worldwide net revenues to U.S. net revenues; that is, we also used estimates of 1.5 and 2.0 in a sensitivity analysis.

All these data were combined to calculate a profitability index frequently employed in the finance literature—the ratio of discounted net revenues to capitalized R and D costs. This ratio, which we label PI, was calculated for each drug. Clearly a PI equal to one implies a project that just breaks even in terms of what alternative invest-

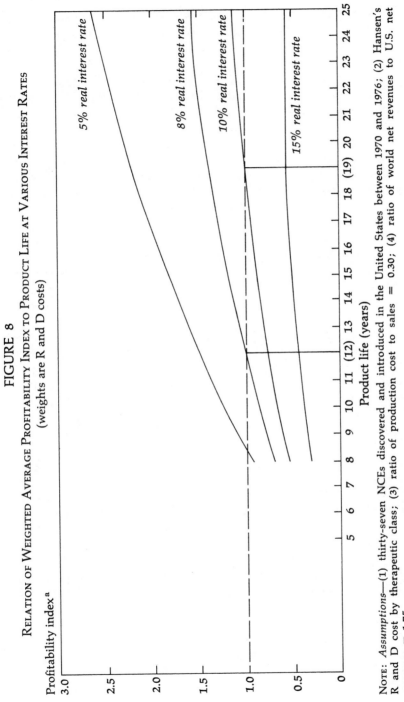

FIGURE 8

RELATION OF WEIGHTED AVERAGE PROFITABILITY INDEX TO PRODUCT LIFE AT VARIOUS INTEREST RATES

(weights are R and D costs)

NOTE: *Assumptions*—(1) thirty-seven NCEs discovered and introduced in the United States between 1970 and 1976; (2) Hansen's R and D cost by therapeutic class; (3) ratio of production cost to sales = 0.30; (4) ratio of world net revenues to U.S. net revenues = 1.75.

a. (Present value of net revenues)/(present value of R and D cost).

SOURCE: Authors.

53

ment opportunities of comparable riskiness are earning and what would be needed to cover long-run investment financing costs from market sources.

In figure 8 the weighted average profitability index for these thirty-seven drugs is shown as a function of expected commercial lifetime, given four different values for the real interest rate or cost of capital for R and D investments. These are in effect break-even product lifetimes. The figure indicates that it takes nineteen years of projected net revenues at current rates to achieve a real return on capital of 10 percent. If we assume that the appropriate real cost of capital (including a risk premium) is 8 percent, the product life necessary to break even is twelve years. These estimates assume that the ratio of production costs to sales is held at 0.30 and that the ratio of world net revenues to U.S. revenues is 1.75.

Since the assumptions about production costs and foreign sales are uncertain, figure 9 was prepared to reflect this uncertainty. Given the probability distributions shown in figure 9, a band of one standard deviation in width about the weighted average PI is presented. The one-standard-deviation band brackets the break-even life between approximately fourteen and thirty years.

Figure 10 focuses on a different type of uncertainty. It shows a frequency distribution of the PIs of the thirty-seven NCEs. The distribution is highly skewed, only thirteen of the thirty-seven projects breaking even or better. The letters are codes for the innovating firms and indicate that firm A had three "winners," while ten different firms had the remaining ten.

Our results therefore indicate that only roughly one-third of the NCEs introduced had a profitability index greater than one. This suggests that a majority of new drugs introduced in the early 1970s have not covered their full R and D investment costs (when allowing both for discovery costs and for the large attrition rate on new product candidates). In effect, pharmaceutical firms are heavily dependent on obtaining a big winner to cover total R and D costs and generate a required return on R and D investments.

Thus a basic finding of our baseline study is that the median return to drug R and D is relatively low, although a small number of big winners earn several times average R and D costs. This result is consistent with an earlier study by Virts and Weston, which also observed a high degree of skewness in the pharmaceutical innovation returns.[5] These results imply that pharmaceutical drug research is comparable to oil exploration and other such activities with above-average riskiness.

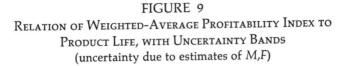

FIGURE 9

RELATION OF WEIGHTED-AVERAGE PROFITABILITY INDEX TO
PRODUCT LIFE, WITH UNCERTAINTY BANDS
(uncertainty due to estimates of M,F)

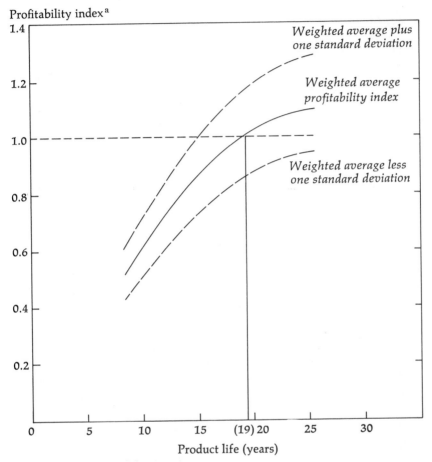

NOTE: *Assumptions*—(1) thirty-seven NCEs discovered and introduced in the United States between 1970 and 1976; (2) real interest rate = 10 percent; (3) Hansen's R and D costs by therapeutic class; (4) ratio of production cost to sales, M, and ratio of world net revenues to U.S. net revenues, F, have following probabilities:

Probability	M	F
0.25	0.20	1.50
0.50	0.30	1.75
0.25	0.40	2.00

a. (Present value of net revenues)/(present value of R and D cost).
SOURCE: Authors.

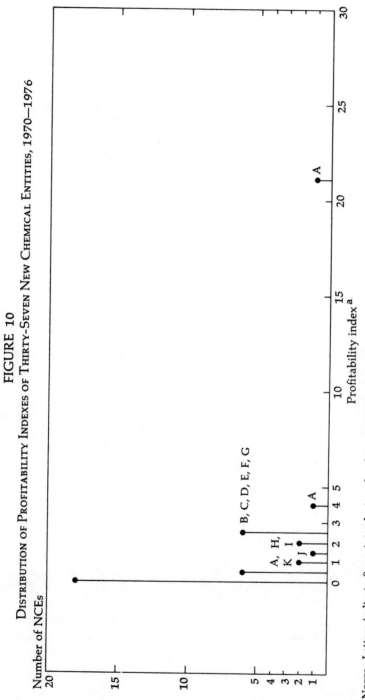

FIGURE 10

DISTRIBUTION OF PROFITABILITY INDEXES OF THIRTY-SEVEN NEW CHEMICAL ENTITIES, 1970–1976

NOTES: Letters indicate firms introducing the thirteen NCEs with PIs $\geq$ 1. *Assumptions*—(1) ratio of production cost to sales = 0.30; (2) ratio of world net revenues to U.S. net revenues = 1.75; (3) Hansen's R and D costs by therapeutic class; (4) real interest rate = 10 percent; (5) product life = twenty years.

a. (Present value of net revenues)/(present value of R and D cost).

SOURCE: Authors.

Sensitivity Analysis Results

The required product life necessary for firms to earn back their R and D investments shown in figures 8 and 9 can be usefully compared with the data on average effective patent life given in table 10. The range of the payback period for the 1970s tended to exceed by a considerable margin the average expected patent life, which was below ten years in 1979. Moreover, the downward trend of patent life tends to increase the divergence over time.

The extent to which declining patent life is a serious disincentive to innovation depends, of course, on how much product competition and substitution actually develop after a patent expires. Such competition can be expected to increase significantly in future periods as a result of the new product selection laws and other institutional shifts favoring low-cost suppliers, although the exact magnitude of such changes is uncertain. If substitution laws significantly increase the market share of imitative drugs, the length of patent protection is critical to the profitability of drug innovation. A shorter effective patent life brings the effect of drug substitution forward in time, increasing the effect of revenue losses on the expected return to innovation.

We can show the sensitivity of the expected profitability of R and D to changes in the effective patent life and the degree of substitution by using the profitability index (PI) analysis in the preceding section. We use the same sample and take as our benchmark case a product life of twenty years and a real interest rate of 10 percent. The PI corresponding to these assumptions is 1.029.

To study the sensitivity of this PI of 1.029 to changes in the effective patent life and the effect of substitution on net revenues, we imposed selected values of these parameters on our data and recalculated the PIs. The results for all cases are given in table 12.

As one would expect, the calculated PIs are lower for shorter effective patent lives and for greater percentage reductions due to substitution. Under the most unfavorable conditions for R and D activity considered here—an eight-year patent life and a 50 percent reduction in U.S. net income—the rate of return is reduced to 0.863, or by about 16 percent from the 1.029 benchmark. When a 30 percent net income reduction and a twelve-year patent life are assumed, the PI is 0.974, or roughly a 5 percent reduction due to substitution. These estimated effects are not negligible and, other things constant, may be expected to make some R and D projects no longer attractive to pharmaceutical manufacturers.

The results in table 12 underscore the fact that the effects of

TABLE 12

PROFITABILITY INDEX FOR ALTERNATIVE ASSUMPTIONS ABOUT THE
EFFECTS OF SUBSTITUTION AND THE EFFECTIVE PATENT LIFE

Percentage Reduction in U.S. Net Income upon Patent Expiration	Effective Patent Life		
	Eight years	Twelve years	Seventeen years
10	0.996	1.011	1.023
	(3.2)	(1.7)	(0.6)
30	0.930	0.974	1.011
	(9.6)	(5.3)	(1.7)
50	0.863	0.937	0.998
	(16.1)	(8.9)	(3.0)

NOTES: The standard against which the profitability indexes (PIs) should be compared is 1.029. This is the PI for a twenty-year commercial life with no reduction in U.S. net income. It is assumed (1) that the ratio of production cost to sales is 0.30, the ratio of world net revenues to U.S. net revenues 1.75, and the real interest rate 10 percent; and (2) that at the end of the effective patent life, substitution will result in the reductions in U.S. net income shown for the remaining years of the twenty-year commercial life. The numbers in parentheses are the percentage reductions for each PI from the standard PI of 1.029.
SOURCE: Authors.

substitution on R and D returns are highly sensitive to the length of patent protection. If the patent life for drugs equaled the legal life of seventeen years, the effects of increased substitution on R and D returns would be quite modest. With a seventeen-year life, a 50 percent reduction in U.S. net income due to substitution causes R and D profitability to decrease by only 3 percent. As patent lives decrease, the effects of drug substitution are magnified.

The analysis in table 12 is undertaken in terms of the expected returns from R and D. This should be a principal influence on R and D investment outlays. In another paper we have undertaken a statistical analysis of the determinants of pharmaceutical R and D investment.[6] Our analysis indicates that firms do respond to higher or lower returns from R and D in the expected manner, but the adjustment process is a gradual one. We also found a statistically significant positive relation between firms' R and D outlays and the availability of internally generated investment funds—another factor adversely affected by declining patent life and increased substitution rates. For the firms in that sample (the major investors in R and D), a $1 million increase in cash flow was associated on average with an increase in R and D expenditures of $250,000. This relation was quite robust over the twelve-year period (1963–1975) we analyzed.

Summary and Policy Implications

Patent protection in pharmaceuticals has been declining, not as a result of conscious policy decisions but as the indirect result of longer clinical development and regulatory approval times. Our analysis of returns on new drug introductions in the 1970s further indicates that these returns are highly skewed. Firms are thus strongly dependent on a relatively small number of major new drugs—those capable of winning large market shares here and abroad to finance the returns on their overall portfolio of R and D investment projects. These major products, however, also provide the most attractive markets for generic follow-on producers. The degree of competition from these firms is likely to increase substantially in the new marketing environment characterized by drug substitution laws and maximum allowable cost programs. Our sensitivity analysis shows that the combination of shorter patent lives and increased substitution would significantly shift the overall distribution of returns from innovation in a negative direction.

Bills restoring patent life for industries subject to premarket approval have been introduced recently in both branches of Congress. For ethical drugs this proposed legislation would add back to the patent life, at the time of FDA approval, time lost during clinical testing and NDA regulatory review, up to some maximum amount. A bill of this kind, S. 255, passed the Senate in June 1981, but failed to gain passage in the House of Representatives during the ninety-seventh congressional session.

The idea of patent restoration has received bipartisan support. President Carter's domestic policy review on industrial innovation recommended patent life restoration for the full class of products now subject to premarket review (ethical drugs, food additives, pesticides, and certain medical devices).[7] It has been strongly endorsed by the current secretary of health and human services, Richard Schweiker, and was favorably reviewed in the past by the former secretary, Joseph Califano.[8]

The analysis undertaken here indicates that patent restoration should have a significant positive effect on R and D investment outlays. It would operate to shift the expected returns schedule from new drug innovation upward and provide firms that are successful in new product introductions with increased profits and cash flow. It should increase R and D investments for both these reasons. Its benefits in this regard would, however, have to be weighed against its costs in the added delays in the availability of cheaper substitute products to consumers.

FIGURE 11

RELATION OF WEIGHTED-AVERAGE PROFITABILITY INDEX TO PRODUCT LIFE FOR ALTERNATIVE
NEW DRUG APPLICATION APPROVAL TIMES

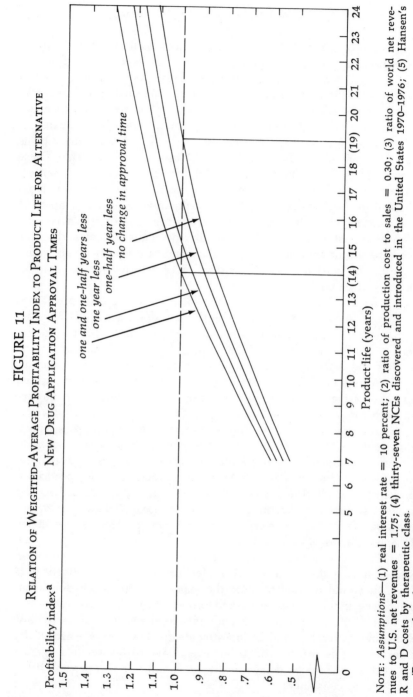

NOTE: *Assumptions*—(1) real interest rate = 10 percent; (2) ratio of production cost to sales = 0.30; (3) ratio of world net revenues to U.S. net revenues = 1.75; (4) thirty-seven NCEs discovered and introduced in the United States 1970–1976; (5) Hansen's
a. (Present value of net revenues)/(present value of R and D cost).
SOURCE: Authors.

Patent restoration is sometimes viewed as a means of offsetting the regulatory-induced delays in new drug innovation. Although this may be a way to justify patent restoration, it is important to note that patent restoration cannot be a complete substitute or offset (at least on a one-for-one basis) for time and resources used up in the regulatory process because it influences only the later years of product life. Many products will be supplanted by rival firms' introductions before the period of patent restoration comes into play. Furthermore, the economic value of time added at the end of the patent period would be much less than that of time restored at the beginning of product life (through, for example, reduced regulatory approval time), because the economic value of dollars obtained in the future is less than that of current dollars (that is, because of the time value of money).

The importance of this point can best be illustrated by the mean profitability index curve. Elsewhere we have analyzed how this curve would be shifted if regulatory approval time were reduced from the 2 years or so that it now averages to 1½, 1, or ½ years).[9] We found that a 1½-year reduction in the time it takes for a new drug application to be approved would reduce the time it takes for a drug firm to recoup its R and D investment by a full five years—from nineteen years to fourteen. This is shown in figure 11, where the analysis focuses on the baseline case, with the cost of capital assumed to be 10 percent. Similar findings occur when other parameters are used in the model.

If one can reduce the "up front" costs and delays associated with regulation, therefore, that will have a much greater effect on economic incentives than comparable gains in patent life added at the end of the exclusivity period. The advantage of patent protection as a policy instrument, of course, is that it can be accomplished through legislative fiat. Shortening regulatory delays and eliminating cost inefficiencies are much more difficult. Nevertheless, our analysis in figure 11 indicates that regulatory reform should continue to be a high priority even if patent restoration is enacted. The next chapter considers some of the main reform proposals.

Notes

1. For further discussion of substitution issues, see Henry G. Grabowski and John M. Vernon, "Substitution Laws and Innovation in the Pharmaceutical Industry," *Law and Contemporary Problems* (Winter-Spring 1979).

2. Henry G. Grabowski and John M. Vernon, "A Sensitivity Analysis of Expected Profitability of Pharmaceutical R & D," *Managerial and Decision Economics* (March 1982).

3. Ronald W. Hansen, "Pharmaceutical Development Cost by Therapeutic Categories," University of Rochester Graduate School of Management Working Paper No. GPB-80-6, March 1980.

4. Celia Thomas, "The Returns to Research and Development in the Pharmaceutical Industry," Ph.D. diss., Duke University, 1981.

5. John R. Virts and J. Fred Weston, "Returns to Research and Development in the U.S. Pharmaceutical Industry," *Managerial and Decision Economics* (September 1980).

6. Henry G. Grabowski and John Vernon, "The Determinants of Research and Development Expenditures in the Pharmaceutical Industry," in Robert B. Helms, ed., *Drugs and Health* (Washington, D.C.: American Enterprise Institute, 1981).

7. Advisory Subcommittee on Patent and Information Policy, Department of Commerce Advisory Committee on Industrial Innovation, Draft Report Proposal VIII (December 20, 1978).

8. Address by Joseph A. Califano, Jr., Secretary of Health, Education, and Welfare, Public Citizen Forum (October 5, 1977).

9. Grabowski and Vernon, "A Sensitivity Analysis."

5

Public Policy Developments and Recommendations

In this final chapter we examine recent proposals for regulatory reform of the FDA as it affects the pharmaceutical industry.

Recent Initiatives

In 1978 the Carter administration introduced parallel bills in the House of Representatives and the Senate that would have comprehensively overhauled all stages of the drug regulatory process. This legislation came to be known as the Drug Regulatory Reform Act of 1978. The Food and Drug Administration under former Commissioner Donald Kennedy played a major role in formulating the substance of this regulatory reform measure. Some of its features were explicitly designed to speed up the introduction of new drugs. For example, the "breakthrough drug" provision would have allowed the conditional introduction of major new medicines into the market while their final testing was still being performed. At the same time, many other provisions of the Drug Regulatory Reform Act would have significantly expanded FDA regulatory powers over new drug development and marketing.[1] Accordingly, many observers felt that overall it would slow down the rate of new introductions. A significantly amended version of the original bill passed the Senate but was never reported out of committee in the House; thus the bill died when the Ninety-sixth Congress expired.

With the installation of the Reagan administration in January 1981, primary attention shifted from legislative to administrative reform of the drug regulatory process. The new administration announced its intention of examining all the major regulations that have evolved from the broad statutory authority granted under the Food, Drug, and Cosmetic Act and its amendments. It opted for administrative reform as its initial strategy in the pursuit of a speedier and more efficient drug regulatory system.

In October 1982 the administration published in the *Federal Register* its first proposed rule changes dealing with the new drug application phase of the approval process for new drugs.[2] Specifically, these new regulations would (1) provide a revised format for NDA submissions, (2) substitute data summaries for the raw case data in NDAs, (3) encourage regulatory review decisions within mandated times, (4) permit greater reliance on foreign data, and (5) change the process for appealing and resolving scientific disputes between the FDA and applicants. New regulatory rules on the investigational new drug (IND) process are scheduled to be published in 1983.

These rule changes address various procedural problems and inefficiencies of the existing regulatory situation and form a logical starting point for the administration's reform efforts. These changes, though meritorious, are unlikely to have dramatic effects on new drug approval times or costs. The FDA's impact analysis indicates an expected reduction in approval times on the order of two to six months from implementing these procedural changes.[3] These new regulations are, however, only the first of several measures under active review.

An Analysis of Current Reform Proposals

In this section we consider some of the major proposed policy changes in the drug regulatory process that have been discussed in recent academic and government studies and task forces.

More Flexible Controls over Early Clinical Trials. Regulatory delays in the early stages of clinical research can especially increase resource costs and time because of the uncertain, recursive nature of the research process. Generally about ten substances are tested clinically for every one that is taken through full development to an NDA. The information garnered from testing the unsuccessful compounds on a small number of individuals in phases 1 and 2 provides a cumulative feedback that is incorporated in successful drug therapies. Delays in the early stages of the clinical process therefore have a compound effect on outcomes and tie up the most creative part of a firm's research organization.

In addition to the controls exercised by the FDA in the IND process, clinical trials are approved and supervised by institutional review boards when they are performed at medical centers. The safety record in these early trials is very good because of the intensive monitoring and their highly controlled nature. Cardon, Dommel, and Tumble of the National Institutes of Health have reviewed the data on injury to research subjects and concluded, "the data suggest that risks of participation in nontherapeutic research may be no greater than those of everyday life and in therapeutic research, no greater than those of treatment in any other setting."[4]

Several recent studies of the drug process, including the General Accounting Office study and the staff report of the House Subcommittee on Science, Research, and Technology, have recommended decentralizing primary responsibility for early clinical trials into the hands of institutional review boards. Under one frequently recommended arrangement, the FDA would issue general regulations and then certify certain health institutions, such as research hospitals, to approve and supervise phase 1 and 2 clinical investigations. The FDA would retain oversight authority, however, to revoke any drug investigations approved by these delegated institutions.

While there is considerable sentiment for delegating more authority over early clinical trials to the institutions where they are performed, there is some question whether these institutions would welcome the added responsibility, which would expose them to added risks of liability suits. Hence it is not clear whether many would accept the full burden of evaluating early clinical trials without any FDA review. This concern would have to be addressed in any policy change of this kind.

Reduced Premarketing Standards of Evidence Combined with Increased Postmarketing Surveillance. As discussed earlier, drug regulation in the current system has an all-or-nothing character. Before approval drugs are restricted to small patient populations under highly controlled experimental conditions. After approval use often increases with minimal regulatory surveillance. Under such circumstances, it is not surprising that regulatory officials tend to err on the side of conservatism in approving new drugs. At the same time, many of the adverse side effects of drugs, those that occur with frequencies of less than 1 in 1,000 or over a longer term, can realistically be discovered only after a drug has been used by large numbers of patients.

The FDA's conservatism before marketing approval has manifested itself in an evolving expansion of its interpretation of what constitute "adequate and well-controlled" investigations of a drug's effectiveness. This frequently puts investigators at the FDA in the position of delaying a drug's entry into the market until the "pivotal" scientific studies are performed, even when there is little doubt about its safety or effectiveness and when it offers significant advances over existing therapies. Furthermore, low-incidence risks (those occurring less than 1 per 1,000) cannot generally be detected in these pivotal clinical studies. The best way to detect them is through more extensive and effective postmarketing surveillance.

An alternative approach to the current all-or-nothing system of drug approval would be to allow new drugs on the market sooner, requiring fewer premarket tests of safety and efficacy, and to expand postmarketing surveillance after the drugs enter the marketplace. This approach is favored by a large number of academic and medical experts as a principal means of getting new drugs to patients sooner while maintaining present safety objectives. There is less than complete consensus, however, on how to change existing procedures to accomplish this general objective. Some specific proposed changes are discussed further in the next two sections.

Conditional Release of New Drugs. A concept that has frequently been advocated in the literature is a conditional approval process for new drugs. New drugs could be marketed when significant evidence of safety and efficacy became available, subject to continued testing and monitoring and FDA authority to stop product sales quickly if warranted. Some of the variants of this proposal would restrict initial marketing to particular institutions or particular medical specialties.

There are precedents for this type of regulatory approval. The FDA has granted some important drugs (for example, L-DOPA) early release for marketing on the condition that manufacturers monitor and report effects on a given number of patients. In addition, the NIH, with its network of clinical centers, has something like a conditional availability of promising new anticancer drugs before formal approval by the FDA for marketing. This involves liberal use of the IND procedures to undertake treatment of dying patients. It is not typical in other therapeutic areas.

The Drug Regulatory Reform Act of 1978 contained a provision allowing the conditional release of "breakthrough" drugs for use in life-threatening, severely disabling, or severely debilitating situations. This provision would have relaxed the standard of evidence from "substantial" to "significant" to allow patients access to such breakthrough drugs while final testing on them was being performed. The statute was designed, however, to restrict the discriminatory use of this provision to a small portion of new drugs.

This approach was criticized in hearings for its narrowness of application and also because it relied heavily on the FDA's judgment to determine whether a drug constituted a breakthrough. The FDA initially classified valproic acid, for example, as a moderate therapeutic advance while the NIH Anti-Epileptic Drug Program was actively campaigning for its rapid approval as a significant advance over established therapies. It was also argued that scientific advances in drugs, as in other fields, are more often incremental and accumulate only gradually to major gains in social welfare. This has been the case historically, for example, in antihypertensive therapy and combination chemotherapy for cancer. Furthermore, the breakthrough status of a new drug sometimes becomes apparent only after it is in general use and often for a purpose different from that originally intended (for example, the diuretic qualities of the sulfa drugs). These factors often make forecasting of the significance of medical advances difficult.

In a larger sense, all drug approvals are conditional, in that some characteristics of new drugs (rare side effects or those occurring after long latency periods) cannot be observed from limited samples in premarket testing. The size and range of possible benefits of a new therapy are also not fully foreseeable or predictable from premarket testing. One needs to make a decision under uncertainty that adequately balances the type 1 and type 2 errors discussed in chapter 1.

As noted in previous sections, we believe the most fundamental cause of drug lag and excessively high R and D expenditures and gestation times for new drugs is an incentive structure that makes regulators more sensitive to type 2 error than to type 1 error. This has resulted in a more restrictive interpretation of the substantial evidence criteria than is required by the statute. To deal effectively with this problem, however, one has to change the incentives faced by FDA personnel. This is discussed in the final section.

Use of Outside Advisers to Make Scientific Decisions. One recommendation frequently made to alleviate these problems is to give a greater decision-making role to expert advisory committees. The GAO notes that this is a positive aspect of several foreign regulatory systems, where greater reliance on outside experts has traditionally occurred than in our system.[5] Such committees bring highly respected academic scientists into the process and thus augment the FDA's internal resources. These advisers are likely to balance benefits and risks more representatively than career civil servants, and their recommendations can serve as an important buffer between the agency and various political groups and advocates. The House subcommittee report also calls for the establishment of an ombudsman within the FDA for promoting and tracking the progress of new drugs and maintaining good communications with industry, consumer protection, and health groups.

The FDA has outside advisory committees for each major therapeutic area, as discussed in chapter 2. Nevertheless, it appears that these committees are often used after the fact to ratify decisions already made by FDA officials. Moreover, participation on these committees has been severely restricted by the Justice Department's interpretation of conflict-of-interest laws. The current interpretation is that even a scientist who has no ties to an FDA-regulated firm but who is affiliated with a university that receives research support from such a firm (for example, under an IND study) cannot serve on such a committee without a special exemption. This restrictive interpretation frequently disqualifies most of those with the greatest expertise and experience.

Outside scientific advisers have frequently been recommended as a logical group to hear appeals concerning scientific disputes between the FDA reviewers and sponsoring firms. Such an appeals mechanism exists in many other countries. In the United Kingdom, applicants can appeal an adverse decision of the Licensing Committee to the Medicine Commission, a fourteen-member body composed of scientists, physicians, veterinarians, and representatives of the pharmaceutical industry. In contrast, the appeals mechanism in the United States involves an internal hierarchical review. This will remain true even under the recent procedural reforms announced by the Reagan administration, which call for the formation of an agency appeals committee to hear major unresolved disputes. Outside advisers will be asked to serve on this committee at the discretion of the director of the Bureau of Drugs, but it appears that the committee will be made up mainly of agency officials and chaired by the director.[6]

In sum, while increased use of outside advisory committees has frequently been recommended as a means of encouraging a more balanced incentive structure and of augmenting existing internal scientific expertise and resources, their potential has been largely unrealized. In many cases they have served as an additional regulatory layer that a new drug approval must hurdle. In a few notable cases, such as sodium valproate, the advisory committees have played an important role in getting the FDA to speed new therapies into the marketplace, but this appears to be the exception rather than the rule.

Regulatory Review Procedures. A detailed analysis of the NDA approval process was performed by the GAO as part of its comparative study in 1980. Although more than 90 percent of all NDAs are eventually approved, approval takes an average of two to three years. The GAO cited the following problems in FDA procedural reviews: (1) FDA guidelines are imprecise, (2) reviewers of the NDA change, slowing the process, (3) scientific and professional disagreements between the FDA and industry are slow to be resolved, (4) FDA feedback to industry about deficiencies is slow, (5) chemistry and manufacturing control reviews are especially slow, and (6) industry submits incomplete NDAs.[7]

As discussed above, the initial administrative rule-making reforms have essentially been addressed to these kinds of management problems. The FDA's strategy has been a combination of less paperwork (that is, through data summaries), parallel agency reviews of applications, mandated times for making decisions, and well-specified and speedier mechanisms for resolving scientific disputes. While this appears to be a well-thought-out and coherent set of procedural changes, its objectives remain very modest. The FDA has estimated that the successful implementation of all these changes will result in a two- to six-month gain in net approval time for new drug entities. Review times are still projected to be much longer than in other developed countries, such as the United Kingdom, where the average approval time is only five months.[8]

A related administrative reform that may have greater quantitative effect in speeding the introduction of new drugs is the greater acceptance by the FDA of foreign data. Several studies indicate that the most severe drug lags have occurred for new drug therapies discovered or developed in foreign countries.[9] Before 1975 the FDA did not accept foreign data at all as positive evidence in support of an NDA's approval. Since that time it has begun to accept foreign data, but the usual requirement is that at least two U.S. studies be conducted to supplement and verify foreign evidence.

In its October 1982 submission to the *Federal Register*, the FDA proposed that new drug approval solely on the basis of foreign data be allowed in some cases, specifically, that drugs with exceptional health benefits, drugs for rare diseases (orphan drugs), and drugs with very low inherent risks be eligible for such approval. At the same time, the FDA appears unwilling to rely solely on foreign data as a matter of general policy because of possible medical, genetic, and cultural differences among countries, the lack of familiarity of the FDA with foreign clinical investigators and facilities, and its inability to conduct on-site verification of most foreign studies.

Although the U.S. position on foreign data has become steadily more liberalized, it is apparently going to remain somewhat more restrictive than that of Great Britain, where the governing consideration is the quality of the data rather than their source. The new U.S. rules will allow much more discretion in the use of foreign data than in the past. It remains to be seen how this discretion will be exercised.

Regulatory Reform in Broader Perspective

The desired regulatory reforms emerging from several recent studies and task forces have several common themes. These include deregulation of early clinical trials and delegation of responsibility over them to institutional review committees, a more balanced weighing of premarket evidence on benefits and risks, greater use of external experts, speedier administrative decisions, and increased postmarketing surveillance.

The administration's current reform initiatives encompass a comprehensive review of FDA regulatory rules and management procedures and possibly extensive changes in them. Although this may be a good strategy for accomplishing some needed reforms in the short run, we doubt whether a rewriting of the administrative regulations coupled with reorganization will lead to very large or permanent changes in the FDA's regulatory approach. As we noted in chapter 1, the FDA's very conservative approach to new drug approval has strong historical roots. Its regulatory mandate emerged in response to highly publicized drug failures and is drawn in very narrow terms: to protect consumers from unsafe or ineffective drugs. As we have emphasized, the incentive to avoid a type 2 error (approval of a bad drug) far outweighs the incentive to avoid a type 1 error (rejection of a good drug). This fundamental asymmetry in incentives seems very difficult to change through new regulatory rules and organizational changes.

The administration has opted to begin with the least controversial reform measures. It should be relatively easy, for example, to increase the acceptability of foreign test data as positive evidence of safety and efficacy through rule making. It should also be possible to eliminate many of the bureaucratic delays and bottlenecks discussed in the GAO report, which contribute to a two- to three-year approval process in the United States compared with five months in the United Kingdom.

A more difficult area to change through rule making is the amount of evidence necessary for FDA medical officers to conclude that a drug is safe and effective. One cannot remove all risks or uncertainties through premarket testing, and some balancing of expected benefits and risks must therefore take place. No matter what the regulatory rules or guidelines concerning acceptable risk say, there will still be strong incentives for FDA officers to avoid risk in interpreting the scientific evidence. They are the ones who must ultimately sign off on approvals of new drugs.

Many countries deal with this incentive problem by delegating the scientific evaluations to committees of outside medical experts. This is a current recommendation of many critics of the U.S. system. This approach, however, may not be easy to accomplish administratively given the traditional emphasis of U.S. regulation on the accountability of civil servants and its much greater concern with conflicts of interest. The development of our regulatory institutions has been much more closely bound to a due-process, adversarial, administrative tradition than to a "consensus of scientific experts" approach. It may therefore not be very easy to bend these institutions toward that approach without legislative changes.

In sum, some important regulatory changes can be accomplished through administrative rule making, and that is undoubtedly worthwhile. We also think, however, that it has limitations as a long-run response to the incentive problems inherent in the present system.

A more fundamental kind of regulatory reform could be accomplished through congressional change in the FDA's regulatory mandate. It is possible to envision an FDA regulatory structure that would operate more as a certifier and disseminator of information for the vast majority of new products introduced. In earlier chapters we noted that the primary rationale for FDA intervention was information imperfection or the possible exposure of patients to uncertain or irreversible hazards from a drug that was inadequately tested or that was of questionable efficacy compared with other therapies. To deal with this "market failure" problem, one could require a premarket review of the evidence carried out under government auspices, using scientific experts within and outside the government. This would provide an independent analysis of the drug's claims of safety and efficacy, which could then lead to required disclosure of information in drug labeling and advertising. The process could be designed to have the evaluation completed within a specified time. Manufacturers would have the option to market a new drug even if it failed to be certified by the FDA.

This alternative kind of premarket certification process would be much less subject to the incentives to risk avoidance present in the current premarket approval system. It might be viewed as erring in the direction of too little protection to consumers from unsafe or ineffective drugs, but this is arguable. Significant deterrents to such behavior would remain. All ethical drugs would still need to be prescribed by a practicing physician before being available to patients. Physicians would have to weigh the FDA's evaluation of safety and efficacy (as well as other evidence) before prescribing a particular product. Considerations of liability and long-term reputability would tend to produce significant incentives to prudent behavior on the part of both manufacturers and physicians.

Whatever the merits of government certification versus licensing for new drugs, there appears to be little chance that the current Congress will seriously consider shifting to the former approach. There is no real political constituency for this kind of change now. There is too much uncertainty about the outcome of an information dissemination program for new drugs, as well as an understandable tendency by all the principals involved to embrace the protection against risks afforded by the current system. Not only FDA officials but the vast majority of physicians, patients, and drug firms appear to favor retention of the system of government premarket approval for new drugs.

Any legislative changes in the current system therefore are likely to be incremental and evolutionary. From the various reform proposals and concepts discussed earlier, two ideas merit special consideration in our view. They are (1) the creation by Congress of a "probably safe and effective" category for the provisional acceptance of new drug products and (2) a shifting of at least some of the legal burden of proof to the FDA for negative actions on NDAs (or inaction after a reasonable time has elapsed). Specifically, the applicant would have the right to appeal any decisions to an external body of scientific experts, which would operate like a scientific court of appeals.

The "probably safe and effective" classification would apply to drugs that have undergone significant testing or possibly market use abroad but for which the "pivotal" scientific studies have yet to be completed. A drug classified as probably safe and effective could be provisionally marketed, provided it was clearly labeled and promoted as such to physicians and patients. As final testing results and new evidence from use by patients became available, the FDA would change the classification to either safe and effective (that is, full approval) or not safe and effective (in which case the drug's provisional approval would be withdrawn).

The reason for this legislative change is that several years now typically elapse from the time a significant amount of evidence exists that a drug has a favorable benefit-to-risk ratio until formal FDA approval takes place. We think the benefits of having these probably safe and effective drugs in the marketplace sooner would outweigh any risks associated with provisional acceptance. Of course, many firms might elect not to market drugs so classified until final FDA approval was received, and many physicians might avoid prescribing them. Nevertheless, this would be an option available to drug innovators. We think firms would probably avail themselves of the option for important new therapies, particularly if they have accumulated considerable experience with patients in foreign countries.

A second area that we think warrants legislative reform involves the burden of proof in new drug approvals. As we discussed in chapter 1, before 1962 some burden of proof rested with the FDA. The system was essentially one of premarket notification and review. If the FDA wished to keep a product off the market, it had to take action within a particular time, and some burden of proof rested on it to justify its action.

After 1962 a premarket approval process was instituted, the burden of proof shifting completely to the new drug applicant. No effective checks then existed on the tendency of the FDA officials to order more tests and delay making final decisions. The total development and approval times for new drugs increased dramatically after 1962, as we showed in chapter 2. We believe the very different incentive structure at the FDA was a major factor in contributing to the long development periods and delays in approving new drugs introduced after 1962.

We think some of the burden should again be placed on FDA investigators to justify their negative action or inaction on NDAs. One way to do this would be to create an external body of experts, similar to the Medicine Commission in Great Britain, to hear appeals on NDA decisions. The law could stipulate the right to appeal not only negative decisions but any application that has been outstanding for a significant period of time (say one year) without FDA action. Subjecting FDA decisions (or indecisions) to this external review process would directly alter the incentives to delay decisions on new medicines. It also would create incentives for the FDA to involve outside advisers and experts more integrally in the decision process.

In sum, we think placing some burden of proof on the FDA and allowing for the provisional acceptance of promising new drugs are desirable and feasible legislative changes in the Food, Drug, and Cosmetic Act. This would result in a more flexible system of government regulation for drugs, one that would allow more scope for informed choice by physicians and patients and would be much less subject to the incentives to risk avoidance in the current system.

Notes

1. For an analysis of the various features of these proposed bills, see *Proposals to Reform Drug Regulation Laws*, American Enterprise Institute Legislative Analysis, no. 8, 96th Congress (Washington, D.C., 1979).

2. *Federal Register*, vol. 47, no. 202, Tuesday, October 19, 1982, pp. 46622–66.

3. Food and Drug Administration, Office of Planning and Evaluation, "Preliminary Regulatory Impact Analysis of Proposed Changes to Regulations Governing the Submission and Review of New Drug Applications (Part 314, Title 21)," May 1982, pp. 32–37.

4. Phillipe V. Cardon, F. William Dommel, Jr., and Robert R. Trumble, "Injuries to Research Subjects: A Survey of Investigators," *New England Journal of Medicine*, vol. 295 (September 16, 1976), p. 650.

5. U.S. General Accounting Office, *FDA Drug Approval—A Lengthy Process That Delays the Availability of Important New Drugs*, HRD-80-64, May 28, 1980, p. 34.

6. *Federal Register*, October 19, 1982, p. 46634.

7. General Accounting Office, *FDA Drug Approval*, p. 12.

8. Ibid., p. 7.

9. See, for example, the analysis of this question in Henry G. Grabowski, "Regulation and the International Diffusion of Pharmaceuticals," in Robert B. Helms, ed., *The International Supply of Medicines* (Washington, D.C.: American Enterprise Institute, 1980).

Date Due